DECLARING
THE END
FROM THE
BEGINNING

(Isaiah 46:10)

Gabriel Ansley Erb

Book adapted from 10 Part video Series "2028 END OF THE WORLD" – now available on DVD or Blu-ray.

This book is currently being translated into French and Chinese. If you know English and another language, and would like to help in translating this book, please contact us at address below.

We are determined to take this final warning message into all the world at any and all cost. If you'd like to purchase these books in bulk to hand out, please use the order information on the last pages of this book.

God help us while we still have day to work (John 9:4)!

ISBN-13: 978-1-7332105-0-8
ISBN-10: 1-7332105-0-4

Printed in the United States of America

10 Love Commandments Ministries
PO Box 814
Nashville, TN 37076

www.2028End.com

gabrielansley@gmail.com

Table of Contents

CHAPTER 1

Introduction

Have you ever wondered when Jesus is going to return to planet Earth? It seems like every year someone is coming up with some reason why THAT year will be the year. Harold Camping thought it would be May 21, 2011. We were told the Mayan's had Dec 21, 2012 pegged as an earth-shattering day. Mark Biltz thought four lunar eclipses in 2014/2015 would be significant. Jonathan Cahn told us the Shemitah year of 2016 would be important. And this year (2017) people were all caught up in a star alignment happening on Sept 23. They thought it would fulfill a sign in Rev 12. And so people were proclaiming the Lord's going to return Sept 23, 2017.

I mean, it's crazy! People are saying things every year! But you know what? The truth about when Jesus Christ is going to return has been known ever since the year 2008! It's been over a decade now! And it's contained in the book I wrote back in 2008 entitled *"Undeniable Biblical Proof Jesus Christ Will Return to Planet Earth Exactly 2,000 Years After the Year of His Death"*. Listen, Christ died on Feast of Passover in the year AD 28 on our calendars today, and he's returning on Feast of Trumpets AD 2028 – 2,000 years later. It's that simple.

So I'm going to reveal this revelation to you right now in this book. And this is going to be the most fascinating information you have ever learned about God's Word. I mean this stuff is going to blow you away! And here's the deal – it's simple! It's easy to understand. There's no difficult math. There's no complex numbers or equations to solve. Einstein realized, "When the solution is simple, God is answering." Well friend that's exactly how it is with this prophetic revelation of Christ's return Feast of Trumpets 2028. It's so simple that it screams out – THIS IS TRUTH!

So I'm inviting you to take a journey with me into the prophetic side of God's Word and the amazing revelation that God has always planned for His son Jesus Christ to return to planet Earth exactly 2,000 years after the year he left it. And if you'll listen to me, I promise you'll no longer be tossed back and forth by every false word people speak each year – trying to pump you up and convince you that Jesus is returning that year. Instead, you'll be like me, grounded and rooted in the prophetic truth of God's Word. Listen, Harold Camping's 2011 Judgment Day date didn't bother me, because I knew the truth in 2008. And I knew the Mayan calendar 2012 date would be a flop. And the blood moons and Shemita years of 2014 - 2016 – it was just hype. And this year (2017) the supposed Rev 12 sign – it wasn't. I had no anxiety about it. And you know why? Because again, I've been grounded in the prophetic truth of God's Word since

2008! So none of these things troubled me, and I don't want people troubling you anymore.

So listen, my name is Gabriel Ansley Erb, and just like the angel Gabriel in the Bible was sent to deliver messages from God to mankind ... well I've been sent to deliver a message to you! So hear me, Jesus Christ is NOT going to return to this planet until the 2,000[th] year arrives after the year of his Death. Christ is returning just one time – Feast of Trumpets 2028. And I'll prove that to you in this book.

CHAPTER 2

The Game of Life

People ask me from time to time, "What's it all about Gabriel? Why are we here? And if there's a God, why did he create planet Earth? And if He loves us so much, then why did He make hell? And why did He put a poisoned tree in the Garden of Eden, setting us up for failure?" Well, these are good questions, and thankfully I have the answer!

Friend, this whole thing is about a GAME. It's a GAME! Listen, do you remember when you were young, and you'd meet up with some friends? What soon happened? Someone would say, "Hey, let's play a game!" Maybe when you were young it was a game of hide-and-seek, or Tag. And then as you got a little older, maybe it was a game of kickball, or baseball, or something.

So think about this … why did you do that? What made you want to play a game? There are two reasons. 1) You were bored. You didn't have anything to do. So playing a game would take away your boredom, for it would give you something to do. And 2) It was FUN! There's pleasure in it! It's fun competing in a game to see who wins. And even if you didn't feel like playing, it was fun watching your friends play. It still kept you from being bored, because it was fun watching how each play unfolded, what happened, and who won or lost in the end.

Well, friend, that's EXACTLY what it's all about on this earth! God created a game! It's called the Game of Life! And He created it to have something to do and for pleasure. The Bible says: "Thou art worthy, O Lord, to receive glory, honor and power: for thou hast created all things, and for thy pleasure they are and were created" (Revelation 4:11). Wow! Did you hear that! Friend, God is getting great pleasure out of watching the Game of Life be played! Listen, how often do you sit around and watch sports? It's fun to watch, right? Are you evil because you like to watch a game be played? Of course not, well neither is God evil because He likes to watch the Game of Life be played!

Furthermore, are the creators of a game evil? I mean in the end someone has to lose the game, and that loss is going to cause them emotional pain and torment? Take for example the losing team in the Super Bowl – the game of Football – listen, I've seen grown men crumbled on the turf in tears at the end, their hearts tore up from thinking about the missed opportunities and plays they could have made to win the game, but they didn't! So are the creators of the game of football evil because they created a game that can cause this kind of torment? No! It's a game. Win it! God's not evil for creating the Game of Life. It's a fair game for everyone. You have the power to win it – so WIN the game!

This concept of "LIFE" being a "GAME" is hinted at in different places in the Bible. For example, Paul wrote: "Do you not know that in a race all the runners run, but only one gets the prize? Run then in such a way as to win the prize!" (I Corinthians 9:24). See, it's a game! And Jesus told us; "There is rejoicing in the presence of the angels of God over one sinner who repents!" (Luke 15:10). Have you ever jumped up and down rejoicing as you watched one of the players on your team make a great play? Well, that's how God and His heavenly angels do as they watch you make the correct decisions in your life to win the Game of Life! I mean they are pumped! They want you to win!

So look, the Bible says we humans were created in God's image. So since God loves and creates games, we do too! We were made in His image! This is why mankind has created literally thousands of games to play. We got winter games, summer games, x-games, computer games, mobile phone games. I mean our world is FLOODED with games. We have golf, tennis, basketball, baseball, hockey, soccer, football, and it goes on and on. It's like we're obsessed with playing games. That's because it's wired into our soul. God loves games, and therefore we do too. And again, there's nothing evil about it.

Alright, so let's look at the 6 major features that make up a game. And then we'll break down the Game of Life with respect to each.

So the 6 main features of a game are …

1. Playing Field
2. Players
3. Rules

4. Coaches
5. Clock
6. Handbook

So let's look at #1 (Playing Field) with respect to God's Game of Life. This is simple ... the playing field is planet earth! And now you know why God created planet earth. It's the playing field for the Game of Life! Listen, there's nowhere you can go on earth that you're not playing in the Game, from the depth of the oceans to the top of the mountains, nowhere is out of bounds. If you're on earth, you're playing in the Game of life. You have no other choice.

Which leads us to # 2 (Players) – that's us, mankind! We're the players in the Game of Life. God created Adam & Eve, and all their kids, to play the game. So it is US who have the opportunity to win or lose the game. Someone asked me one time, "What's it matter if we win or lose the Game of Life, Gabriel? Doesn't matter, does it?" Wow! Friend, nothing could be further from the truth! Because to win or lose this game has ETERNAL consequences for your soul!

To win the game is to receive eternal life in heaven. You get to live with the creator of the game for all eternity, the great God, the source of all love and light. Let me tell you, it will be joy unspeakable and full of glory! They'll be singing and rejoicing. There's rest, and food, and water. They'll be no more pain, no more sickness, no more tears, no more sorrow. It's almost unimaginable how beautiful, peaceful, and loving it will be for those who win the Game of Life.

But to lose the Game? Friend, you don't want to do that! The losers in the Game of Life will receive hell first and then the lake of fire. It will be eternal separation from the creator God, the source of all love and light. It will be pain unthinkable and full of torment. There will be wailing and gnashing of teeth. They'll be no rest day or night, no food, no water. They'll be intense pain, tears, and darkness. Trust me … you don't want to lose the Game of Life!

And this brings us to #3 (Rules) for playing the Game of Life. This is where God's 10 Love Commandments (10LC) come in! They are the instructions for how to play the Game of Life. Those who live by them (which is to live a life of love towards God and others) will win the game. Those who willfully disobey them, will lose the Game! It's that's simple. Knowing this, you should realize nothing could be more important than you understanding EVERYTHING about these 10 rules from God, for they are the plays you must run to win the Game of Life.

In fact, it's so important that we created an entire website to explain everything about them. It's called www.10LoveCommandments.com. And if there's anything you ever do for yourself on this earth, you should devour everything on that website! There's a *"Salvation Equation"* video series that will clear up salvation (how to obtain eternal life), exposing all the false salvation doctrines in today's churches. And there's a *"10 Love Commandments"* video series, where you can learn everything about God's rules for the Game of Life. I can't urge you strongly enough to watch these two seminars, for the knowledge contained in them has the power to change your life.

Ok, so now we've reached #4 (Coaches) in the Game of Life. I'm going to make this real simple for you ... the Game of Life is played by two teams, like the American game of football. One team's head coach is Jesus, and the others team's head coach is Satan. In other words, everyone on earth is playing for <u>one</u> of those two teams, including you! Jesus' team runs plays of love (they keep the 10LC) while Satan's team runs plays of pride (they disobey the 10LC). Said another way, the players on Jesus' team live by the Golden Rule (they treat others as they'd want to be treated), but the players on Satan's team do not (they use others for their own selfish gain).

And one more thing about coaches, there are also many secondary coaches in the Game of Life. Jesus has angels, and Satan has demons. And depending on what team you're playing for, these secondary coaches will talk to you in your mind's ear, encouraging you to run plays for their team. Satan's demons will urge you to murder, lie, steal, commit adultery, covet, etc. But Jesus' angels will urge you to forgive, to speak the truth, to give, to honor the marriage bed, to be content, etc. Again, visit our inspiring website www.10LoveCommandments.com to learn all about the plays each of these two teams run.

So now we come to #5 (Game Clock) feature in the Game of Life. Friend, <u>THIS</u> is what this "2028 END" book is about! It's about the game clock in God's Game of Life! Listen, most games have a clock. They're timed. And not only do they have a total time for the game – like 48 minutes for basketball, or 60 minutes for American football – but then that total time is divided up into smaller equal units, like 4 periods for basketball (each of them 12 minutes) or four quarters for football (15 minutes each). Understand?

Well get this … this is <u>EXACTLY</u> how it is with God's Game of Life! From the very beginning, God determined the Game of Life would be played for a total time of 6,000 solar years, beginning to end. But then He divided that total time up into 6 equal periods of 1,000 years each. So that's the game clock, or the timing scenario, for the Game of Life! But then there's one extra thing God did … after the initial 6,000 years is over, there's going to be one more period added to the game (one more 1,000 year period) called the 7th period. Think of it like a bonus period. And after that period is over, THEN the Game of Life will officially be over. That's when all the winners will enter into eternal life in heaven, and all the losers will enter into eternal death in the lake of fire, the second death.

So listen, we're going to talk A LOT more about God's 7 Day (7,000 year game clock) in this book, and I'm going to irrefutably prove to you that it's truth! But for right now, I just wanted to introduce you to the concept of the game clock in God's Game of Life, because this is what the timing prophecies in God's Word are actually all about!

So this brings us to the last main feature #6 (Handbook) in the Game of Life. And for the Game of Life this is simple – it's the Bible! The Bible contains all the information for the Game of Life; it lays out the playing field, the players, the rules, the coaches, and the game clock. I mean it's all there! And we're going to get into the Game Clock portion of it BIG TIME in this seminar!

So just realize, the big questions of life (why are we here, why did God make planet earth, what's it all about, etc) can be answered very easily when you understand this whole thing is about a game. We're all playing in the Game of Life. And winning or losing this Game is going to have eternal consequences for our soul. So God's watching! He's testing you! He wants to see which team you'll choose to play for! And I pray you choose Jesus!

CHAPTER 3

Creation Day 7
Christ's Millennial Kingdom

Alright, since we now know this WHOLE THING is about a game, with a playing field, players, rules, coaches, and a game clock, I want you to think about something ... do you play a game halfway through (or even further) until you know how it's timed? No, you know the timing scenario from the beginning. You're always aware of the game clock. That's only fair.

For example, if you're playing the game of American football, you need to know when you reach the final 2 minutes of the game, because at that point the sense of urgency increases, and you begin altering your play calling to win the game. Well, this is exactly how it is with the Game of Life! God understands "knowing the clock" is part of playing the Game of Life. And therefore, from the Creation of the World, God announced the ending time, as well as how many periods the total time would be divided into. It was all stated from the beginning!

So listen very closely to what I'm about to say ... this is the ENTIRE REASON God used 7 DAYS in the Creation story! He didn't need 6 days to create everything. He didn't need one! He could have created everything in a millisecond, and left it at that. But no, He purposely chose to use 7 Days in the Creation event in order to lay out the timing scenario (or the game clock) for the Game of Life. Listen, if you want to tell time, you have to use numbers, right? Think about it ... time is told with numbers. So this is why God used the number "7" in the Creation story. Right out of the gate, by utilizing 7 Days in the Creation story, God was announcing ... "The Game of Life will be played for 7 periods, and then it will be over!"

It says in the Game of Life's handbook: "I am God, and there is no one like me, DECLARING the END from the BEGINNING" (Isaiah 46:9-10). Wow! See, don't take my word for it – take God's! It's right there in your Bible in black and white – God declared (meaning spoke) the end from the beginning!

So listen, to fully understand this verse you need to understand the ENTIRE 7 Day Creation story is "the beginning". Two verses will prove this. Jesus said, "From the beginning of the Creation, God made them male and female" (Mark 10:6). Jesus was talking about us in this passage, mankind, and we were created on Day 6 of Creation, but Jesus was still calling it "the beginning of the Creation". In other words, what Jesus is really saying here is the Creation story (all 7 days!) was "the beginning". Another time, Jesus said, "He was a murderer from the beginning." (John 8:44). This was about Satan's murder in the Garden of Eden, when he tricked Adam & Eve into sinning in the Garden of Eden, and they died spiritually. This happened shortly after the 7 Day Creation event (the Jews have a tradition where they believe it was 3 days later, or day 10 when this happened) and so Jesus is still rightly calling this event "the beginning".

So listen, what these verses are proving is the 7 Day Creation week was one literal week of time (just like we know a "week" today), and these 7 Days were "the beginning" of God's 7,000 year Game of Life. So if you compare the first week of time to approximately 4,000 years having passed (when Jesus was on earth speaking) ... do you see how that first week would easily be considered "the beginning"? I'm laboring on this point because I want you to understand when God says "He declared the end from the <u>beginning</u>" ... it means He declared the end in the 7 Day Creation story.

This is important to know, because then all we have to do is look for the word "end" somewhere in the Creation story, and we'll know the time of the end! It's really that simple! And guess what? It's there, just one time. It says this: "And on the 7th Day God <u>ENDED</u> His work which He had made; and He rested on the seventh day" (Genesis 2:2). Wait, what? God ENDED HIS WORK WHICH HE HAD MADE? Huh? Isn't that a strange way for God to announce He quit working after 6 days? Friend, that's because it's prophecy! In those cryptic words, God was prophesying, "I'm going to DESTROY what I made!" And when? After 6 Days (or 6 periods) are complete! Upon which the final period will commence, a time of rest, the 7th period.

So listen, the only thing God kept a secret in the Creation story was the length of these periods. The first record we have of it is through Moses in the Game of Life's handbook: "For a thousand years in God's sight are but as a single day that passes" (Psalms 90:4). In other words, each Creation Day represented (or FORETOLD) a FUTURE 1,000 year period! God then confirmed this truth again through Peter: "But, beloved, be not ignorant of this one thing, that one day is with the Lord as a thousand years, and a thousand years as one day" (II Peter 3:8). By the way, don't overlook how God prefaced that statement with ... be NOT IGNORANT of this! God was saying ... I'm about to say something very important, so PAY ATTENTION! And it was important, for God gave out the "key" to the length of the 7 periods He declared in the Creation story – each Creation day foretold of a future 1,000 year period!

Well friend, when Jesus left planet Earth, after his resurrection, and he sent the Comforter (whom he said would lead us into all truth) ... it didn't take long for the Holy Spirit to start revealing to the early church fathers the 7 Day Creation story foretold of a 7,000 year plan God had for Earth. And they knew the "end" would come after 6 Days (or 6,000 years) which would be Christ's 2nd Coming. And they knew that event would be followed by a restful 1,000 year Sabbath period on Earth, in fulfillment of Day 7 in the Creation story [See Figure 1]. This millennial Sabbath would be the earthly reign of Jesus Christ with all the saints. John wrote about it in the Game of Life's handbook in Revelation: "Blessed and holy is he who has part in the first resurrection (Christ's 2nd Coming) ... for they shall be

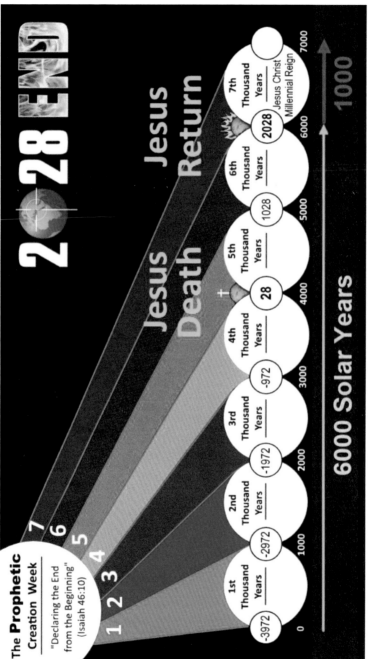

Figure 1 - God's 7 Day / 7,000 Year Plan

priests of God and of Christ, and shall reign with Him a thousand years" (Revelation 20:6). Hallelujah!

And listen, this (7 Creation Day / 7,000 year) doctrine was not some odd doctrine known by only a few in the early church. No, it was wide spread! They all knew it! Listen to the words of the early church fathers ...

Barnabas wrote: "He speaks of the Sabbath at the beginning of the Creation, 'And God made in six days the works of His hands and on the seventh day He made an end, and He rested on the seventh day, and He sanctified it.' Consider, my children what this signifies: That He made an end in six days. The meaning of it is this: that in six thousand years the Creator will bring all things to an end, for with Him one day is a thousand years. He Himself testifies, saying, Behold the day of the Lord shall be as a thousand years. Therefore children, in six days, that is in six thousand years, all things shall be accomplished. And He rested on the seventh day: He means this, that when His Son shall come He will destroy the season of the wicked one, and will judge the godless, and will change the sun and the moon and the stars, and then He will truly rest on the seventh day. (Epistle of Barnabas 15: 3-5, 70 - 130 AD)

Irenaeus wrote: For in as many days as this world was made, in so many thousand years shall it be concluded ... This is an account of the things formerly created, as also it is a prophecy of what is to come. For the day of the Lord is as a thousand years; and in six days created things were completed; it is evident therefore, that they will come to an end at the six thousandth year. (Irenaeus 150 AD - was trained by Polycarp who was trained by John who wrote the Book of Revelation. Quote is from "Against Heresies" Book 5, 28, 3)

Hippolytus wrote: And six thousand years must be accomplished, in order that the Sabbath may come, the rest, the holy day "on which God rested from all His works." For the Sabbath is the type and emblem of the future kingdom of the saints, when they "shall reign with Christ," when he comes from heaven, as John says in his Apocalypse: for "a day with the Lord is as a thousand years." Since, then, in six days God made all things, it follows that six thousand years must be fulfilled. (Hippolytus – 170 - 235 AD)

And Lactantius wrote: Therefore, since all the works of God were completed in six days, the world must continue in its present state through six ages, that is, six thousand years. And as God laboured during those six days in creating such great works, so His religion and truth must labour during these six thousand years, while wickedness prevails and bears rule. And again, since God, having finished His works, rested the seventh day and blessed it, at the end of the six thousandth year all wickedness must be abolished from the earth, and righteousness reign for a thousand years; and there must be tranquility and rest from the labours which the world now has long endured. (Lactantius 240 - 320 AD - Tutor to the son of the Roman Emperor Constantine, was a highly respected scholar. He wrote sometime before his death in 330 A.D. the following in "The Divine Institutes" Book 7, Chapter 25)

Wow! So there you go! This 7 Day / 7,000 Year plan of God is rooted in history! This is not something new! The early church fathers were absolutely convinced God had <u>PURPOSELY</u> utilized 7 Days in the Creation event in order to "declare the time of the end from the beginning." And specifically, to announce the end is coming after 6 days/periods (earth's 6,000 year) followed by Christ's 1,000 year Sabbath reign. So just think ... for 20 centuries now this 7 Day / 7,000 Year plan of God has been known and taught by God's prophets!

This reminds me of an incredible encounter I had back in 1983, when I was just a young boy, 12 years old. I have to tell you this story. My dad had seen an ad in the newspaper about a "traveling prophet" who was going to speak in a church that we had never visited. Dad was curious what a "prophet" was today. You have to understand our family had only been going to church for 2 years at this time. So we didn't know much!

Well we went, and near the end of the prophet's message that night, he walked back the center aisle, pointed at me, and said, "Stand up, son! Do you know God gave you your name? For it is Gabriel!" (He had my attention with that!) He continued, "Son, God's placed the creativity of 4 men inside of you. And you will be like John the Baptist in the last days preparing the people to meet the Lord, for God is going to place you in a position one day to be able to influence multitudes of people!"

Wow! I sat down, bewildered. My head was spinning. Yet, I never forgot the words he spoke over me! It's like they were permanently engraved in my mind. I mean think about it, I was only 12. And I never wrote them down. Yet I've never forgotten what he said. And I never tried to self-fulfill the words. I just lived my life. I finished high school. I went to college majoring in Chemistry & Biochemistry. I wanted to be a doctor. And then in my mid 20's, of all things, I decided to move to Nashville, Tennessee to be a country music singer! Crazy! So as you can see, I wasn't trying to make the prophets words be true in my life!

But then one night in 2005, here in Nashville, when I was 34 years old, God performed a miracle for me that was so stunning ... it jolted God back to first place in my heart and mind. I mean the miracle was so amazing that all I could think about day and night was "How did God do that?" And let me tell you, it drove me to seek God and His Word like never before in my life! It began a 2½ year journey that ended with God giving me a message for the world about the Bible that is mind-blowing. And you can read all that in my 2008 book "Undeniable Biblical Proof Jesus Christ Will Return to Planet Earth Exactly 2,000 Years After the Year of His Death".

But back to the prophet who called me out when I was 12 ... guess what his message was that night? Would you believe he was preaching God's 7 Day Creation story foretold of a complete 7,000 year plan He had for planet earth! I remember it like it was yesterday! He had a big chart up front on an easel showing it. And since it was 1983 (and he knew Ussher's 4004 BC Creation date), he knew earth's 6,000 year was soon coming around the year 2000.

Let me explain something to you about this 7 Day / 7,000 year prophecy ... a lot of preachers (for no reason at all!) had it in their head that the year of Christ's BIRTH was earth's 4,000 year. The prophet didn't say that that night, but I learned of this recently. So if you believe Christ BIRTH was year 4000 (which is near year 0 on our Gregorian calendar) then obviously right near AD 2000 was earth's 6,000 year. Many prominent prophecy preachers today believed this! And so in AD 2008 I heard them all begin abandoning God's 7 Day/7,000 year truth! They began preaching Earth's 6,000 year had now come and gone, even though obviously Jesus had not returned! I was flabbergasted! They were tossing aside 20 centuries of God's prophets! Shocking!

But I'm here to tell you ... these modern day "prophets" are wrong! For it was NOT the year of Christ's BIRTH that was earth's 4,000 year ... it was the year of his <u>DEATH</u> (on the cross) that was earth's 4,000 year!!! And God prophesied this fact over TEN TIMES in His Word! But sadly, throughout history, no one knew it! But God revealed these things to me in AD 2008, the year I wrote my book, and I'm going to reveal them to you in this book. Jesus DIED in the year AD 28 on our calendar (which was earth's 4,000 year) and he will return AD 2028 (which will be earth's 6,000 year)! It's that simple.

So here I am in 2019, preaching the same message the prophet was preaching who called me out when I was 12, just in more detail! Listen to me; God's 7 Day / 7,000 year plan for this earth is alive and well! It's still in effect! Twenty centuries of prophets were not wrong! Earth's 6,000 year has not come yet! It will arrive in AD 2028. The prophet said over me in 1983 ... "God's going to place you in a position one day to influence multitudes" ... Well, here I am on the internet, making videos and writing books, reaching millions of people. We made a 2028 END movie in 2014 that now has almost 10 million views. We're sending books and posters around the world. We have 3 websites revealing the stunning truths of God's Word. It's amazing to me what all God's done. And even more amazing ... the words of that prophet back in 1983 were all true!

So look, this is where God's 7 Creation Day / 7,000 Year Plan has stood now for 20 centuries. They've known Day 7 in the Creation story was prophetic about earth's 7th millennium. They knew the words "rest" and "sanctification" in that day (to set apart as holy) were prophetic words about the "rest" and "holiness" that will exist during the 1,000 year reign of Christ on earth, when Satan will be locked up in the bottomless pit [See Figure 2].

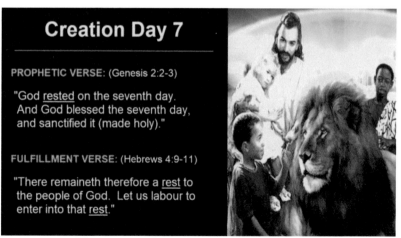

Creation Day 7

PROPHETIC VERSE: (Genesis 2:2-3)

"God rested on the seventh day.
And God blessed the seventh day,
and sanctified it (made holy)."

FULFILLMENT VERSE: (Hebrews 4:9-11)

"There remaineth therefore a rest to
the people of God. Let us labour to
enter into that rest."

Figure 2 – Creation Day 7 Prophecy

But are you ready for this … here's what they didn't know! In other words, here's what we have no written record of anyone ever knowing throughout history! Are you ready? It wasn't just Day 7 in the Creation story that contained prophetic words about its future millennium – it was all 6 days before it!!! EACH day in the Creation story contained prophesy about its future millennium! In other words, Day 1 of Creation contained a prophecy about what would happen during earth's first 1,000 years. Day 2 of Creation contained a prophecy about what would happen during earth's second 1,000 years. And on and on! And these weren't just little meaningless events that were prophesied. No, these were HANDS DOWN THE BIGGEST EVENTS to occur during each respective millennium in God's plan for this earth! Friend, when this is learned, I don't know how anyone could deny the truth of God's 7 Day / 7,000 year plan for planet Earth! This prophetic information cements God's 7 Day / 7,000 year plan as truth!

So this is what the next 6 chapters of this book are going to be about. We're going to go through each Creation Day, and I'm going to reveal to you the hidden prophetic words contained in each about their respective future millennium. And I pray the world wakes up to these truths, and preachers begin teaching it all over the world. People need to know the Game Clock for God's Game of Life is quickly running out!!!

CHAPTER 4

Creation Day 1
Adam & Eve's Fall

Alright, to summarize where we're at … we learned in chapter 3 that God's prophets have been proclaiming (for almost 2,000 years now!) that God <u>purposely</u> chose to use 7 Days in the Creation event in order to declare the time of the end from the very beginning. And this was accomplished through the fact that each of those 7 Creation days foretold of a future 1,000 year period, for a total 7,000 year plan God had for planet Earth. And the prophets knew the 7th Day Sabbath in the Creation story foretold of Christ's 1,000 year Sabbath kingdom on Earth, which would arrive at Christ's 2nd Coming Earth's 6,000 year. And this is where the revelation stood for the past 2,000 years.

But in AD 2008 God began to show me that it wasn't just Day 7 in the Creation story that contained prophetic words about its future millennium, it was all 6 days before it! Each Creation day contained a prophecy about the biggest event to occur during its respective future millennium. So Creation Day 1 prophesied about Earth's first 1,000 years, Creation Day 2 prophesied about Earth's second 1,000 years, and on and on. So we're going to get into this revelation right now, starting with Day 1 of Creation, and I'm going to show you the words God used in that day's events in order to secretly prophesy the fall of Adam & Eve in the Garden of Eden, which was by far the biggest event God had planned to occur during Earth's first 1,000 years.

But first, do you remember the words Irenaeus wrote in the second century? You read them in the last chapter. He said: "The Creation story is an account of the things formerly created, as also it is a prophecy of what is to come." Man, he didn't know how right he was! He didn't know EACH Creation Day contained a prophecy about the biggest event to occur during its future millennium! And yet he still wrote those words! Amazing!

By the way, God actually confirmed this is all true with these words: "I am God, and there is no one like me, Declaring the End from the Beginning, and from ancient times the things that are not yet done, saying, My plan will take place, for I will do all my will" (Isaiah 46:9-10). Wow! Did you hear that? So not only did God declare the time of the end from the beginning, but He's saying He declared things that were not yet done! He called it "from ancient times" but realize God spoke these words through Isaiah around 800 BC. So "ancient times" in 800 BC would likely mean the Creation event.

The great John Wesley did a commentary on the Bible in the 1700's, and he knew what Isaiah 46:10 was saying, even though He didn't fully understand how God had done it. He said "God was foretelling from the beginning of the world, future events which should happen in succeeding ages, even to the end of the world. Wow! That is exactly what I'm going to reveal to you in this book!

So let's look at the first day of Creation and see (as John Wesley put it) the "event" that God foretold to happen during Earth's first millennial age. Day 1 of Creation reads like this ...

> In the beginning God created the heaven and the earth.
>
> And the earth was without form, and void; and darkness was upon the face of the deep. And the Spirit of God moved upon the face of the waters.
>
> And God said, Let there be light: and there was light.
>
> And God saw the light, that it was good: and God divided the light from the darkness.
>
> And God called the light Day, and the darkness he called Night. And the evening and the morning were the FIRST day. (Genesis 1:1-5)

So what's the hidden prophecy in these words? It's the line "God DIVIDED the LIGHT from the DARKNESS" (Genesis 1:4). Friend, these words foretold the fall of Adam & Eve in the Garden of Eden! Let me explain.

Do you see in the narrative God called the light "good"? Well, by default this is like calling the darkness "evil". And in fact, throughout the Bible, God confirmed this analogy of light being good and darkness being evil. Jesus said: "And this is the condemnation, that light is come into the world, and men loved darkness

27

rather than light, because their deeds were evil. For everyone that does evil hates the light, neither comes to the light, lest his deeds should be exposed" (John 3:19-20). So you see darkness is likened to evil and light as good. Paul wrote: "For you were once darkness, but now are you light in the Lord: walk as children of light. For the fruit of the Spirit is in all goodness, righteousness and truth ... have no fellowship with the unfruitful works of darkness, but rather reprove them" (Ephesians 5:8-11). See there it is again, light as good and darkness as evil.

So looking back at the words in Genesis 1:4, where it says "God DIVIDED the Light from the Darkness" it was prophesy foretelling Good & Evil would be divided sometime during Earth's first 1,000 years! And friend, this is EXACTLY what happened when Adam & Eve sinned in the Garden of Eden.

The forbidden tree in the Garden was called the tree of the KNOWLEDGE of GOOD and EVIL! God told them: "But of the tree of the knowledge of good and evil you shall not eat, for in the day that you eat of it you shall surely die" (Genesis 2:17). Well they ate of it! And they died that very day, spiritually! And their eyes were opened, and for the first time in their lives they knew the difference between what was good and what was evil. God made this pronouncement: "Behold, man has become like one of us, knowing good and evil" (Genesis 3:22). Do you see it? Good & Evil was now DIVIDED in mankind's hearts! They knew the difference between them!

So understand Genesis 3:22 is the fulfillment verse for what God had prophesied to happen in Genesis 1:4

[See Figure 3]. In other words, get this ... when Adam & Eve sinned, Bible prophecy was already being fulfilled! Did you hear that? Just think, four verses into the Bible and God is already prophesying! It's shocking! And if you'd do a careful study of the prophetic verses Christ fulfilled during his first Coming, you'd see what I'm telling you about Genesis 1:4 is the truth. You'd see it's just like God's other prophetic words in Scripture. For He moves in and out of prophecy so quickly and smoothly that it's breath-taking!

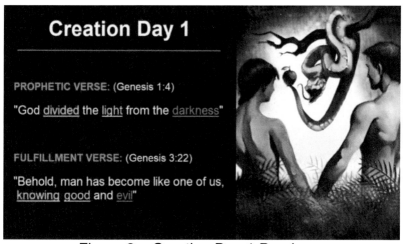

Figure 3 – Creation Day 1 Prophecy

By the way, if you just think about light & darkness in the physical sense (like what God was literally creating on Day 1 of Creation) it really makes no sense to have to say "God DIVIDED the light from the darkness". Think about it, where there's light it just naturally expels the darkness. They don't need to be divided, it just happens! Turn on a lamp in a dark room ... and boom! ... the light instantly pushes back the

29

darkness and fills the room. So saying God DIVIDED the light from the darkness appears like a throwaway line. It really doesn't make much sense physically. In other words, you could remove that line from Creation Day 1's narrative and everything makes sense without it ... "And God said, let there be light: and there was light. And God called the light day, and the darkness he called night. And the evening and the morning were the first day" (Genesis 1: 3-5). Makes perfect sense!

But listen, when you understand God wanted to PROPHESY "things that were not yet done" from the beginning of time ... then the line takes on a whole new meaning and significance! I am telling you the truth, the words "God divided the light from the darkness" in Creation Day 1's narrative were secret prophesy about the biggest event to occur during Earth's first 1,000 years – the fall of mankind into sin and its resulting death! In fact, the event was so important that it completed the setup of God's Game of Life! Remember what we talked about in chapter 2? Listen, once mankind was under the "death penalty" for sin, the option to lose the Game of Life was now on the table! In other words, God's gameboard for the Game of Life was now fully open, and it was GAME ON for all mankind!

Remember the guy who asked me, "Come on Gabriel, why would God put a poisoned tree in the Garden of Eden, setting us up for failure?" Well now you know! It was to set up the option (or the choice) for mankind to now either LOSE or WIN the Game of Life! It's that simple! It's just like I told you in chapter 2 of this book – it's ALL about a game!

30

Ok, so now you know WHY God prophesied the fall of mankind in Day 1 of Creation. He knew it was going to happen during earth's first 1,000 years! He needed it to happen to finish the set up to His Game of Life! It's like we read earlier in Isaiah 46:10 "God's PLAN will take place (which means He has a plan!) for He will do all His will." Amen to that.

Alright, so there's one last thing I want to tell you, just briefly here in chapter 4, because most people don't understand this (even church people!) ... and yet it's REALLY important to know ... when Adam & Eve learned the difference between Good and Evil, what it actually means is they learned the 10 Love Commandments (10LC). This is a powerful revelation! ALL "goodness" is defined by "obedience to the 10LC, and ALL "evil" is defined by disobedience to the 10LC. It's that simple. So Adam & Eve learned (knew) the 10LC the moment they ate from the tree of the knowledge of good and evil. How cool is that?

If you read my book "*Undeniable Biblical Proof Jesus Christ Will Return to Planet Earth Exactly 2,000 Years After the Year of His Death*" you'll notice I point out story after story in the book of Genesis proving mankind knew the 10LC long before God wrote them on stone tables at Mt Sinai. Mankind has always known them! They are the ONLY difference between what is good & what is evil! Good gives, evil steals; good forgives, evil hates; good is content, evil covets; and on and on with them. Visit our wonderful website www.10LoveCommandments.com and you can learn all about the 10LC and how they are the COMPLETE LIST of ALL good & evil thoughts, words, and deeds.

So that's all I'm going to say about that for now, but just realize, God has been perfectly fair to all mankind from the very beginning of time, for He supplied them with the ONLY KNOWLEDGE they needed to know to win the Game of Life (meaning obtain eternal life) – namely, follow the path of good (keep 10LC) and shun the path of evil. And "The Salvation Equation" video series on our www.10LoveCommandment.com website will really help you understand all of this.

Alright, so to sum up where we're at … we now know God prophesied the fall of Adam & Eve in Day 1 of Creation, and this event was fulfilled during earth's 1st millennium, likely year 1. And we know God prophesied of Christ's soon-coming restful and holy Sabbath Kingdom in Day 7 of the Creation story, which will be fulfilled during Earth's 7th millennium. So next we're going to reveal God's secret prophetic words in Day 2 of Creation foretelling the greatest event He had planned to occur during Earth's 2nd millennium!

CHAPTER 5

Creation Day 2
Noah's Global Flood

Alright, so now we've come to Day 2 of Creation. And you know what we're doing … we're revealing the secret prophecies God made in EACH creation day foretelling the greatest event to occur in that day's future millennium. So Creation Day 2 foretold of earth's 2nd millennium.

Remember, the ONLY REASON – hear me, the ONLY REASON!!! – God used 7 Days in the Creation story was to be able to declare the time of the end from the beginning. Time is told using numbers. So each of the Creation Days foretold of a future 1,000 year period, for a total 7,000 year plan God had for planet Earth. And to leave no doubt this is truth, God did something astounding! He hid prophecies in the wording of each creation day's events foretelling the greatest event to occur in that day's future fulfillment millennium! And this is the greatest revelation of our time! If everyone learned these prophetic truths in the Bible, it would change the world!

So here we are at Creation Day #2. God hid words in this day's events to secretly prophesy the global Flood of Noah's day! And then the Bible carefully confirms this event took place during Earth's 2nd 1,000 year period. It's truly fascinating! But why was the flood event so important? In other words, why would God want to prophesy of it in Day 2 of Creation? It's because the entire story of Noah, the Ark, and the global flood was one massive, real-life, prophetic parable about Jesus Christ's 2nd Coming and the end of the world. Friend, the story of Noah is prophecy that's not yet been fulfilled! God even declared in the story – AGAIN! – that the "end" will come Earth's 6,000 year! So this will be the second time He's prophesied this fact, the first one being in the Creation story as we already learned in chapter 3.

Ok, so Creation Day 2's narrative reads like this ...

And God said, <u>Let there be a firmament (sky) in the midst of the waters</u>, and let it divide the waters from the waters.

And God made the firmament, and divided the waters which were under the firmament from the waters which were above the firmament: and it was so.

And God called the firmament Heaven. And the evening and the morning were the <u>SECOND</u> day. (Genesis 1:6-8)

Did you notice there's a lot of water talked about in this day's events? That's not by accident! So what are the secret prophetic words foretelling the global flood of Noah's day? It's the line "Let there be a SKY in the

MIDST of the WATERS" (Genesis 1:6). Friend, these words prophesied of the flood, for that was the first time it would rain on the earth. In other words, that was the first time the sky was full of water. The sky was in the midst of the waters!

Listen, until the flood event happened, it had never rained on Earth. The Bible says: "There went up a mist from the earth, and watered the whole face of the ground." (Genesis 2:6). But at the time of the flood, the Bible says: "The fountains of the great deep burst open, and the floodgates of the sky were opened. The rain fell upon the earth for forty days and forty nights" (Genesis 7:11-12). There's your fulfillment verse … during the worldwide flood the skies were in the midst of the waters for the very first time.

So Genesis 7:11 is literally the fulfillment verse for what God had prophesied to happen in Genesis 1:6 [See Figure 4]. Pretty amazing! And even if you're of the camp where you believe rain fell on earth before Noah's flood, just understand the global flood event was the first and only time the earth's ENTIRE SKY was in the midst of water. In other words, the entire expanse of sky surrounding the earth contained rain. THIS is the fulfillment of what God prophesied in Day 2 of Creation.

So let's confirm Noah's flood took place during earth's second 1,000 year period. It's remarkable that we even have this information! But God was careful to include the birth ages of the patriarchs from Adam to Noah, and then Noah's age when the flood happened, so that we can know the EXACT year the flood happened from Creation. Now why would God do this?

Friend, it's so we'd have proof of the things I'm telling you today! It's so you would know, without a doubt, that Noah's story happened during earth's second millennium, perfectly fulfilling Creation Day 2's prophecy.

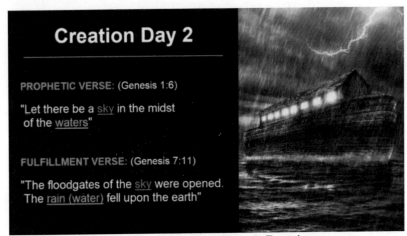

Figure 4 – Creation Day 2 Prophecy

So here's a chart [See Figure 5] showing the birth ages of the fathers. You can get this information in chapters 5 & 7 of Genesis. And it's easy to add up. You'll see Adam was 130 years old when Seth was born, and Seth was 105 years old when Enosh was born, and so forth. And if you add it all up (which doesn't take long) you'll learn Noah was the 10th father from Adam, and he was born in the year 1,056. Then the flood event happened 600 years later, which was year 1,656. So it's very clear in the Bible that the story of Noah, the Ark, and the Global Flood ALL happened during earth's 2nd millennium, which runs from years 1,000 to 2,000!

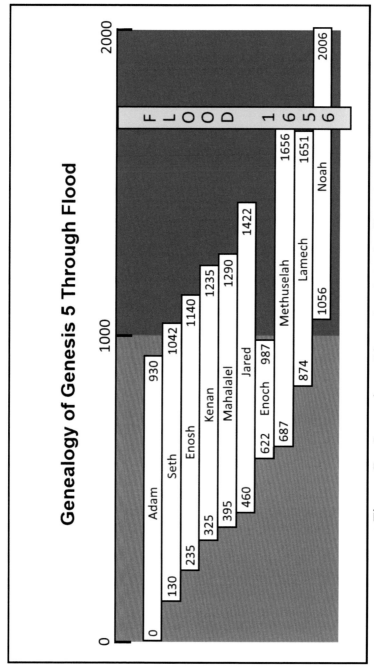

Figure 5 - Genealogy Chart 1st & 2nd Millennium

So now for the fun part! What about the story of Noah, the Ark, and the global flood? What's so special about it? Why would God want to prophesy of it in Day 2 of Creation? In other words, why was it going to be the greatest event of earth's 2nd millennium? It's as I told you earlier, it's because the entire story was itself a prophecy about the end of the world, meaning Christ's 2nd Coming! Try and grasp this fact ... the story of Noah, the Ark, and the global flood contained the details of HOW the end of the world would unfold, back in a time when the Bible wasn't even written yet!!! Think of that!

So I told you earlier the story is a real-life prophetic parable. Now listen, when you normally think of a parable you think of the <u>spoken</u> word. Someone just speaks a parable, like Jesus would. But this is different. This is God literally controlling the events of a REAL LIFE story that happened on Earth, so that the details and events of the story are parabolic, delivering a PROPHETIC message to mankind! I don't know about you, but I don't know of any other being in the universe that can do something like this! It's mind-boggling.

So since it's a parable, let me tell you what the things in the story represent – Noah represents Jesus and the Ark represents heaven. So Noah is going to be a prophetic picture of Jesus, and the Ark he's building is going to be a prophetic picture of the literal place of heaven. Four details in the story prove the Ark represents the place of heaven.

1. God tells Noah: "with lower, second, and third stories shall you make it" (Genesis 6:16). Later, Paul

informed us "I knew a man in Christ … who was caught up to the <u>third</u> heaven" (II Corinthians 12:2). This is the only time in the Bible we're told heaven has 3 stories. So there's a 1st, 2nd, and 3rd heaven, exactly like God told Noah to build in the ark.

2. God told Noah: "Make <u>rooms</u> in the Ark" (Genesis 6:14). Later, Jesus came along and said, "My Father's house (meaning heaven) has many rooms" (John 14:2). These words from Jesus were affirming the parabolic truth of the story of Noah – the Ark was a picture of heaven. And since God knew heaven has rooms, God wanted Noah to make rooms in the Ark.

3. God told Noah: "You shall make a <u>window</u> for the Ark" (Genesis 6:16). Later, God said, "Prove me, if I will not open the windows of heaven and pour out a blessing for you" (Malachi 3:10). See it? Heaven has windows, so God wanted Noah to put windows in the Ark.

4. God told Noah: "Put a <u>door</u> in the side of the Ark" (Genesis 6:16). Later, Jesus came along and said, "I am the door. If anyone enters through me, he will be saved" (John 10:9). See, Jesus is the <u>ONLY</u> DOOR that leads into heaven; therefore, God wanted Noah to build only one door in the side of the Ark.

So there you have it, it's undeniable the Ark in the story of Noah is a precise picture of the place of heaven. It's the ONLY place of safety that exists from the coming end of the world destruction! So do you see what's happening in the story of Noah? As Noah worked building the Ark, he was a <u>prophetic</u> picture of Jesus building the place of heaven. Remember Jesus saying, "I go to prepare a place for you. And if I go and prepare a place for you, I will come again, and receive you unto myself; that where I am, there you may be also" (John 14:2-3). Friend, Noah is the picture of that! As he built the 3 stories in the Ark, as he built each room in it, as he built the windows and the one door, he was a picture of Jesus preparing the place of heaven for us. And as I said, it's the ONLY place of safety that will exist when the global end-of-the-world destruction comes about!

So when the destruction was finally at hand in the story of Noah, guess who God called into the Ark? Only Noah's family! Him, his wife, his three sons and their wives (his three daughter-in-laws). God said to Noah, "Come thou and all thy <u>house</u> into the Ark; for you have I seen righteous before me in this generation" (Genesis 7:1). Friend, this detail perfectly reveals whose going to be saved when Jesus returns! It will be ONLY be Christ's family! The Bible says: "But Christ as a son over his own house; whose house are we, if we hold fast the confidence and rejoicing of the hope firm unto the end" (Hebrews 3:6). In other words, if you've repented of your sins, and you're fighting the good fight of faith, you are a son or daughter of Christ. And Jesus is the head of this household. So here it is again in the story of Noah; a precise prophetic truth of how the end of the world will unfold – only one house of people (one righteous family) is going to be saved from the destruction, all else, all the wicked people, will perish! And it's the builder's family (the builder of the place of safety) that will be saved – Noah building the ark, and Jesus building heaven

And now for the thrilling action in the story of Noah! This is remarkable because it clearly reveals WHEN the "catching away" of the believers will happen. Watch this … as Noah's flood is taking place, what happens to the Ark (remember it's holding Noah's family). The Bible says: "And the waters increased, and bare up the ark, and it was <u>lifted</u> <u>up</u> high above the earth" (Genesis 7:17). Friend, this is the "catching away" or the "gathering" event of the believers, up into the air! It's what the church calls the "rapture". But they're confused about its timing. Look when it happens … at the SAME TIME as Noah's family is rising up into the air in the ark ALL the wicked people on earth are being destroyed! In other words, there's no more time left for anyone when the "rapture" happens! Do you know what this means; there's NO pre-tribulation rapture event! That's a lie! And the story of Noah proves it!

The believers will be "caught up" into the air on the SAME DAY as all the wicked people on Earth are perishing! Paul says it like this: "Then we which are alive and remain (meaning those of us who are still alive and remaining on Earth, having miraculously made it through 3½ years of the antichrist's reign) shall be caught up together with them in the clouds ("them" is those who have already died in Christ, they'll be returning with Jesus in the clouds) to meet the Lord in the air: and so shall we ever be with the Lord" (I Thessalonians 4:17). This whole event is called the "gathering" in the Bible, for all the believers from 6,000 years of Earth's history will be gathered together on that final day. Those who have already died will be returning with Christ, and those of us still alive and remaining on Earth will be caught up to meet them in the air. And Jesus confirmed when this "gathering" event takes place: "Immediately <u>AFTER</u> the (Great)

Tribulation ... he shall send his angels with a great sound of a trumpet, and they shall GATHER TOGETHER his elect from the four winds, from one end of heaven to the other" (Matthew 24:29-31). So it all happens AFTER the Antichrist's 3½ year Great Tribulation period mentioned in Matthew 24:21.

And here's the final proof in the story of Noah that this whole "gathering" event (and the end of the world) will happen Earth's 6,000 year and not some 7 years before ... The Bible records, "Noah was SIX HUNDRED years old when the floodwaters came on the earth" (Genesis 7:6). Wow! Do you get it? Friend, God carefully controlled Noah's age to be 600 when the flood event occurred to secretly prophesy the end of the world will take place Earth's 6,000 year! So just like one righteous family of people (Noah's house) was "caught up" into the air to safety as a world of ungodly people perished in a flood of water, all when Noah was 600 years old ... so too one righteous family of people (Christ's house) will be "caught up" into the air to safety as a world of ungodly people perish in a flood of fire, all when earth is 6,000 years old. Friend, I am telling you the truth, the story of Noah, the Ark, and the global flood was/is unfulfilled prophecy about the end of the world, and it will be perfectly fulfilled during Jesus Christ's return Earth's 6,000 year AD 2028.

I was awakened around 8am February 27, 2008 to a voice explaining to me all the things I'm telling you about the story of Noah. As you can imagine, my mind was blown! I'd never heard anything like it before in my life! No church ever taught me these things! But I've written them all down in the Noah chapter of my book "Undeniable Biblical Proof Jesus Christ Will Return *to Planet Earth Exactly 2,000 Years After the Year of His Death"*. And it's one of the most fascinating chapters in the book. I don't have time in this short book to tell you everything about the story, but I do in the book. So get it, and read it!

I will point one more thing out though, just briefly … the story of Lot and the destruction of Sodom & Gomorrah contains the EXACT SAME end of the world prophetic message as the story of Noah! In other words, it too is unfulfilled prophecy about the end of the world. Therefore, it too will be fulfilled on the day of Christ's return. And this information is in the Lot chapter of my book. But just realize, in this story the same thing happens … one righteous house of people (Lot, his wife, and his two daughters) are "caught up" out of Sodom by angels (a picture of the "gathering" event) on the SAME DAY as all the wicked people are being destroyed by fire.

And what's really cool is when Jesus came along, he actually confirmed the stories of Noah & Lot were prophetic parables about his return. And if you'll listen closely to his words, you'll hear he confirms what day the "catching away" (or the rapture) occurs. He made a point to say: "The SAME DAY that Lot went out of Sodom it rained fire and brimstone from heaven, and destroyed them all. EVEN THUS shall it be in the day when the Son of man is revealed" (Luke 17:29-30). Do you see it! I believe the Holy Spirit led Christ to say those words exactly like that so the debate between a pre-trib or post-trib "rapture" is over. The rapture is the "gathering" and it happens on the SAME DAY as all the wicked people on earth are destroyed! It's at the end! It does not happen 7 years before the end. That's a lie! Friend, when the "catching away" of the believers happens, that's it! There's no more time to get right with God! It's over! 6,000 years of Earth's history will have been complete, and the surface of planet Earth will be completely destroyed with a flood of fire, as Peter tells us: "But the day of the Lord will come like a thief in the night; in which the heavens shall pass away with a great noise, and the elements shall melt with fervent heat, the earth also and the works that are therein shall be burned up" (II Peter 3:10). See, it's the fulfillment of the story of Lot and the destruction of ALL wicked people by fire!

Now listen, the church today is dreadfully ignorant of these parabolic truths, and therefore it's not speaking them. They don't understand a mass extinction event is coming the day of Christ's return, just like the stories of Noah and Lot. They're clueless! So you're not going to hear these truths from them! But now you know the truth of what's coming and when, Noah's story told it to you – Earth's 6,000 year AD 2028!

And one last thing … after the fire is over and all the wicked people annihilated, God is going to regenerate the surface of planet Earth back into a glorious paradise, where He'll sit all the gathered righteous people back down on it, just like Noah's family was sat back down on the Earth after the global flood. And they'll enter into the glorious 1,000 year Sabbath reign of Jesus Christ in fulfillment of the 7th Day Sabbath in the Creation story!

So there you have it … now you know WHAT God prophesied in Day 2 of Creation concerning Earth's 2nd millennium, and WHY it was such a big deal. I pray it's been a blessing! Next time we're going to disclose what God prophesied in Day 3 of Creation concerning earth's 3rd millennium, and I promise it's every bit as fascinating as Day 2!

CHAPTER 6

Creation Day 3
Moses and Red Sea Parting

So here we are now at Creation Day #3. What did God prophecy in this day's events concerning Earth's third 1,000 year period? Are you ready? He prophesied the parting of the Red Sea event! If you remember, this is the story where Moses stretched out his arms and the Red Sea parted. It's the event where the Israelites passed over to freedom, while the Egyptians perished in the Sea. "Well, ok," you say, "I remember that story, but what's the big deal? Why would God want to prophesy of that event?

Listen close now … it's because the ENTIRE SCENE of Moses "stretching out his arms" at the Red Sea was itself a prophecy, about Christ's death! When Moses stretched out his arms he was a prophetic picture of the Messiah Christ Jesus stretching out HIS arms on the cross and dying for us! So just like the story of Noah is a prophetic parable about Christ's 2nd Coming, so too the story of Moses is a prophetic parable about Christ's 1st Coming.

But here's what's REALLY going to blow your mind ... just like God hid a secret timing detail in the story of Noah to prophesy Christ's return will occur Earth's 6,000 year (remember Noah was 600 years old when the floodwaters came?) well so too God hid a secret timing detail in the story of Moses to foretell Christ's death would occur Earth's 4,000 year! Mind-blowing!

So let's delve into this. Let's learn first how God prophesied the parting of the Red Sea event in day 3 of Creation, and then we'll prove from the Bible that this event happened, without a doubt, during Earth's third 1,000 year period. The narrative reads like this ...

> And God said, <u>Let the waters under the heaven be gathered together unto one place, and let the dry land appear</u>: and it was so.
>
> And God called the dry land Earth; and the gathering together of the waters called he Seas: and God saw that it was good.
>
> And God said, Let the earth bring forth grass, the herb yielding seed, and the fruit tree yielding fruit after his kind, whose seed is in itself, upon the earth: and it was so.
>
> And the earth brought forth grass, and herb yielding seed after his kind, and the tree yielding fruit, whose seed was in itself, after his kind: and God saw that it was good.
>
> And the evening and the morning were the <u>THIRD</u> day. (Genesis 1:9-13)

So where's the prophecy? It's the line "Let the WATERS under the heaven be GATHERED TOGETHER unto one place, and let the DRY LAND APPEAR" (Genesis 1:9). Friend, these words secretly foretold the parting of the Red Sea, because during that event the waters of the Red Sea were gathered together and the dry land appeared.

The Bible records the story like this, "And Moses stretched out his arm over the sea; and the Lord caused the sea to go back by a strong east wind all that night, and made the sea <u>dry</u> <u>land</u> … And the children of Israel went into the midst of the sea upon the <u>dry</u> <u>ground</u>" (Exodus 14:21-22). There's your fulfillment verse! Do you see it? The sea became dry land!

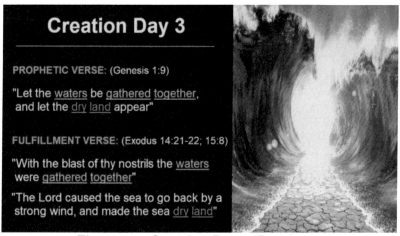

Figure 6 – Creation Day 3 Prophecy

And then there's this verse (just one chapter later!) still talking about the Red Sea event: "And with the blast of thy nostrils the waters were <u>gathered</u> <u>together</u>, the floods stood upright as a heap, and the depths were congealed in the heart of the sea" (Exodus 15:8). Wow! Do you see the word precision God is using here to confirm fulfillment of the prophecy He spoke in Day 3 of Creation? It's literally the SAME words! In both cases, the waters were "GATHERED TOGETHER" and the "DRY LAND" appeared! I mean it's stunning! Exodus 14:21-22 and Exodus 15:8 are the fulfillment verses for what God had prophesied to happen in Genesis 1:9 [See Figure 6]. I am telling you the truth ... God prophesied the parting of the Red Sea event in Day 3 of Creation!

So let's prove this event happened during Earth's third 1,000 year period. Amazingly, God continued to record the birth ages of the patriarchs in the book of Genesis so we would know. So as we look at our chart [See Figure 7] starting with Noah this time, we see Noah was 500 years old when he had Shem (so that's year 1,556 after Creation). Shem then had Arphaxad two years after the flood (so that was Earth's 1,658th year). And if you keep following this out in Genesis chapter 11, you'll learn Abraham was the 20th father from Adam, and he was born in the year 1,948. So he was born near the end of Earth's second 1,000 year period.

Abraham was then 100 years old when he had Isaac, year 2,048. (So now we're into Earth's third 1,000 year period, which runs from years 2,000 to 3,000!) Isaac was then 60 years old when he had Jacob, and God changed Jacob's name to Israel. Jacob's children and descendants ended up in Egypt when he was 130 years old, Earth's 2,238th year. Then the Exodus happened 400 years later, year 2,638. So no question about it ... the ENTIRE story of the

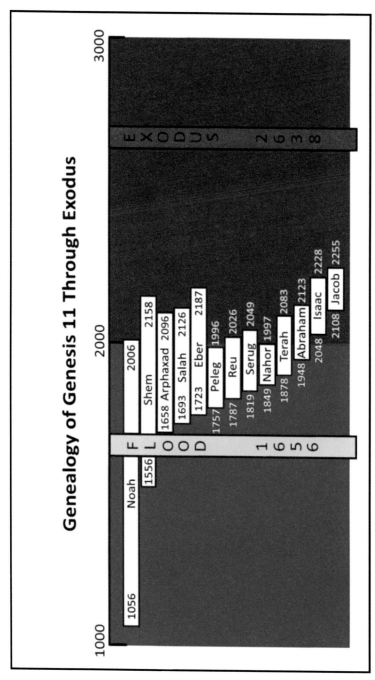

Figure 7 - Genealogy Chart 2nd & 3rd Millennium

Israelites and the "parting of the Red Sea event" happened during Earth's third 1,000 year period.

And listen, I know there are disagreements on how people count the years for the Exodus date. But I challenge you (cause I've looked at them) ... they all agree on this fact ... the ENTIRE story of Moses & the Israelites happened during Earth's 3rd millennium. This truth is undeniable from the Bible. So without a doubt God prophesied the parting of the Red Sea event in Day 3 of Creation, and without a doubt the event happened during Earth's third 1,000 year period, in perfect fulfillment of God's prophetic words!

Alright, so what's the big deal? Why is the parting of the Red Sea event the GREATEST event God had planned to occur during earth's 3rd millennium? It's as I told you earlier, it's because the event itself was a prophecy about the greatest event to ever occur – the Messiah's death on the cross! Listen, what God did for the Israelites through Moses at the Red Sea was a prophetic picture of what God would do for us through Jesus on the cross! Let me say that again ... what God did for the Israelites through Moses at the Red Sea was a prophetic picture of what God would do for us through Jesus on the cross!

Friend, it's a parable! The story of the Israelites is a prophetic parable. Now don't get me wrong ... it's a REAL LIFE story! It really happened on this Earth! But God was carefully controlling the story (its happenings & details) so that those happenings and details had parabolic meaning, delivering a prophetic message to mankind.

So since it's a parable, let me tell you what the things in the story represent. The Kingdom of Egypt represents the Kingdom of Darkness, and Pharaoh represents Satan. Consequently, Pharaoh ruling the Kingdom of Egypt in this story was a parabolic picture of Satan ruling the Kingdom of Darkness. The Israelites in the story represent us, all mankind. Moses represents Jesus (the coming Messiah). And the Promise Land in the story represents Heaven (the place where eternal life can be had).

Now listen carefully, God's whole purpose for creating this story (this real-life parable) was to unveil this message ... <u>Everything Required for Us (Mankind) to Obtain Eternal Life</u>. That's what the story is about! That's its message! God literally crafted this story of the Israelites bondage in Egypt, deliverance through Moses, and wilderness journey to a Promise Land, all for the purpose of delivering the message of ALL messages to mankind – Everything Required for Us to Obtain Eternal Life!

So it's God's salvation message! It's God's central story in the Bible! All 66 books in the Bible point to this story's message and validate its truth. This is the knowledge that is missing in today's church world, and it's the reason demonic salvation doctrines abound. I promise you, if you'll learn God's message behind this story, you'll never be confused about salvation again! You'll have an honest chance at obtaining eternal life! All we have to do is learn what it took for the Israelites to make it to the Promise Land in their story, and we'll know everything it takes for us to make it to heaven!

So let's look at what happened to us (mankind) first: when Adam & Eve sinned in the Garden of Eden, at Satan's coercion, they immediately fell under bondage to sin and its resulting death. (Remember God said, "You eat of the forbidden tree and you will die"). So at that point, Satan became the god of this world, and it was he who held us (mankind) in slavery to that sin and its resulting death. And from that point on, we would ALL sin! And since the "wages of sin is death" (Romans 6:23), then we had no hope of obtaining eternal life. So no heaven! No eternal life! We would all just die on this Earth and go to hell. It was a desperate horrible situation. We were enslaved to sin and death under Satan's power!

So looking at our story of the Israelites, God set up this same situation by enslaving the Israelites in Egypt under Pharaoh's power. (Remember, Pharaoh represents Satan and the Israelites represent us.) So Pharaoh's taskmasters would beat the Israelites, forcing them to do hard labor, and they would die. Oh, the Israelites dreamed of the Promise Land. They wanted to get there. But they had no chance! Pharaoh and his Egyptian army were too strong. (Remember, the Promise Land in the story represents heaven.) So the Israelites would never be set free from their enslavement and make it to the Promise Land. They would all just die in Egypt. It was an exact mirror of our situation – The Israelites enslaved under Pharaoh's power was a parabolic picture of us enslaved under Satan's power. They had no hope of getting to the Promise Land on their own, and we had no hope of making it to Heaven on our own.

So what did God do for the Israelites? He sent them a deliverer. A savior! The man Moses! Remember, Moses represents Jesus in this story. So Moses is going to be the man God will work through to free the Israelites from Pharaoh's power, opening up a way for them to be able to get to the Promise Land. And all of this work of Moses will be prophetic! It's prophecy! Moses is a picture of our deliverer, our Savior, the man Jesus! So God will work through Moses to foreshadow how He will work through Jesus to free us from Satan's power, opening up a way for us to be able to get to heaven!

So I'm going to skip a lot in the story, which you can read in the Moses chapter of my book (chapter 9) *"Undeniable Biblical Proof Jesus Christ Will Return to Planet Earth Exactly 2,000 Years After the Year of His Death"*, because I want to get right to the Red Sea scene, the final scene of deliverance, the parting of the Red Sea, which precisely foreshadowed Christ's work on the cross.

Five things happen here …

1) Moses stretches out his arms
2) The Red Sea divides
3) Pharaoh and his army's power are destroyed
4) The Israelites are saved
5) A way to the Promise Land opens

These 5 things foretold …

1) Jesus would stretch out his arms on a cross.
2) The Temple Veil would divide
3) Satan and his demon's power would be destroyed
4) Mankind would be saved
5) A way to Heaven would open

So on #1, the <u>outstretched arms</u>, God told Moses: "Lift up your staff and stretch out your arm over the sea and divide it, and the sons of Israel shall go through the midst of the sea on dry land" (Exodus 14:6). This pictured the way in which Jesus would deliver us ... with outstretched arms on a cross.

On #2, the <u>dividing of the Red Sea</u>, it says: "Then Moses stretched out his arm over the sea; and the Lord caused the sea to go back by a strong east wind all that night, and made the sea into dry land, and the waters were divided" (Exodus 14:21). This pictured the dividing of the Temple Veil that would happen when Christ died on the cross. The Temple Veil led into the Holy of Holies, the place where God dwelled. So this symbolized a way back to God was opening!

On #3, <u>Pharaoh's power destroyed</u>, it reads: "And Moses stretched out his arm over the sea ... Then the waters returned and covered the chariots, the horsemen, and all the army of Pharaoh. Not so much as one of them remained" (Exodus 14:27-28). This pictured the complete victory Jesus' death would win over Satan while he died on the cross. The Bible says, "Through death, Jesus destroyed him that had the power of death, that is, the devil" (Hebrews 2:14). Friend, Satan's power over us was destroyed the moment Christ's righteous death became <u>available</u> to pay our sin debt. Remember, the "wages of sin is death", but Jesus never sinned! So he paid a death sentence for sin he didn't owe! And now his righteous death sits there <u>available</u> to all mankind to pay our death sentence. That's how Satan's power of death over us was destroyed!

56

So on #4, the <u>Israelites are saved</u>, the Bible reads: "So the Lord SAVED Israel that day out of the hand of the Egyptians, and Israel saw the Egyptians dead on the seashore" (Exodus 14:30). This pictured God would SAVE us out of the hand of Satan, through Christ's death on the cross. The Bible says: "He (Jesus) has saved us and called us with a holy calling" (II Timothy 1:9).

And on #5, a <u>way to the Promise Land opens</u> ... I think you understand! The Israelites were free! The enemy's power over them was destroyed! The way to the Promise Land was now wide open to them! This pictured when Christ died for us, we were free! The enemy's power over us was destroyed! The way to Heaven was now wide open to us! And Christ's righteous death made it possible!

So there you go ... THAT'S God's powerful message behind the story of the Israelites, Moses and the parting of the Red Sea event. It was a parable! And it was all about OUR Messiah, Christ Jesus, and what he would do for us on the cross. THAT'S why it was the greatest event of Earth's 3rd millennium! And that's why God wanted to prophesy about it in Day 3 of Creation!

But there's one more detail (one seemingly small insignificant detail) I want to tell you about the Israelite's story. Why? Because it's actually massive!!! God planned and controlled this detail to happen to <u>secretly</u> prophesy the YEAR of Christ's death on the cross! Hundreds of years earlier God had told Abraham His plans for the Israelites' story, He said, "Know for certain that for <u>FOUR HUNDRED</u> YEARS your descendants will be strangers in a land not their own, and that they will be enslaved and mistreated there. But I will punish the nation they serve as slaves, and afterward they will come out with great wealth" (Genesis 15:13-14). Oh, my goodness! Do you see it? God delivered the Israelites out of Egypt, through Moses' outstretched arms at the Red Sea, after 400 years of bondage! Friend, God controlled this number to prophecy He would deliver us, through Jesus' outstretched arms on the cross, after we'd been in bondage for 4,000 years! In other words, Christ died for us (on the cross) during Earth's 4,000 solar year counted from Creation!

It's just like the story of Noah … God used HUNDREDS of years in both stories (both parables) to prophesy the TIME! Noah was 600 years old when the Flood struck to prophesy Christ's return will happen Earth's 6,000 year. And likewise, the Israelites were delivered after 400 years of bondage to prophesy Christ would deliver us after 4,000 years of bondage. I am telling you the truth … Jesus Christ DIED on the cross during Earth's 4,000 year! And that year was AD 28 on our Gregorian calendars today, which I'll tell you about in chapter 9.

Now before we wrap this chapter up, I want to point out one last truth to you in the Israelite's story (parable). Why? Because this is the most important part of the story to understand! The "wilderness part" of the story – the part the Israelites are now about to go through, where they have to make a JOURNEY to get to the Promise Land? – it contains ALL the answers to what WE must DO to make it to Heaven! Did you hear that? The wilderness part of the story is where the answer lays to what <u>WE</u> (not God!) must DO to obtain eternal life! See God did his part through Moses at the Red Sea! That was His free gift! That was His grace! But now it's OUR turn to do our part!

So do you know what it was? It's the WHOLE REASON for the Mt. Sinai scene in the story. Just 50 days after the Red Sea event, God gathered the Israelites at the base of Mt Sinai and thunderously spoke the 10LC to them. And then He said, "These 10 Commandments which I command you this day shall you observe to DO, that YOU MAY LIVE … and go in and possess the Promise Land" (Deuteronomy 8:1). Wow! And if they would NOT keep them, God said, "I swore in My wrath, they shall NOT enter My rest in the Promise Land" (Hebrews 3:11). Wow! Friend, listen to me, keeping the 10LC has ALWAYS been <u>OUR</u> <u>DUTY</u> in obtaining eternal life! Remember, in chapter 4, we learned the moment Adam & Eve ate from the Tree of the Knowledge of Good & Evil they learned the 10LC? So all mankind has known them! That means everyone has had a choice to obey them or not.

So just understand, obtaining eternal life is a journey! It's a walk! It's not a one-time decision! It's a NARROW <u>WAY</u> that leads to life that few will follow. Why? Because they do NOT want to live a life of love towards God and others as outlined by the 10LC! You think I'm lying? Listen to Jesus' answer when a man asked him, "Good teacher, what must <u>**I**</u> (not God!) DO to obtain eternal life?" He said, "If you want to obtain eternal life, keep the 10LC" (Matthew 19:16-19). Another time he simply replied, "Love God with all your heart and love your neighbor as yourself, DO THIS and you will live!" (Luke 10:25-28). Friend, these two answers are one and the same, because to "love God with all your heart" and to "love your neighbor as yourself" is accomplished ONLY by "keeping the 10 Love Commandments".

Here's the deal, friend ... Jesus knew what the story of the Israelites in the Old Testament was about! He knew its parabolic message! He knew the "wilderness part" of the story held the answer to what WE needed to DO to obtain eternal life (make it into the Promise Land). We need to repent, to turn from our sins (Matthew 4:17)! We need to go and sin no more (John 8:11)! It will be a fight, the GOOD fight of faith (I Timothy 6:12). It will be a continual journey of "working out our own salvation with fear and trembling" (Philippians 2:12). Solomon confirmed this when he wrote; "Fear God, and keep His (10 Love) commandments: for this is the WHOLE DUTY of man" (Ecclesiastes 12:13).

Well friends, I don't know how else to say it ... the story of the Israelite's bondage in Egypt, deliverance through Moses, and wilderness journey to a Promise Land is a real-life parable! It was designed by God to reveal Everything Required for Us (Mankind) to Obtain Eternal Life. It covered God's Duty at the Red Sea and it covers Our Duty in the Wilderness. BOTH are necessary to enter the Promise Land (obtain eternal life). And we've created an entire website to carefully explain all of this to you – it's affectionately called www.10lovecommandments.com. On that site you'll find a 12 part video series entitled "The Salvation Equation" which explains God's message behind the Israelite's story and much more. If you watch that seminar, you'll be completely set free from the demonic salvation doctrines circulating rampantly in today's churches. And then watch "The 10 Love Commandments" series, so you understand how ALL sin is based on disobedience to the 10LC and ALL love is based on obedience to them. Together, these two seminars will completely clear up salvation for you. You'll never be confused again!

So that's it … now you have a basic understanding of God's parabolic message behind the story of the Israelites bondage in Egypt, deliverance through Moses, and wilderness journey to a Promise Land. And now you know WHY the "parting of the Red Sea" event in the story was such a significant event. And you also know how God prophesied in the story that Christ's death would occur Earth's 4,000 year! So all in all, you should have no problem now understanding WHY God prophesied of the Red Sea parting in day 3 of Creation! Nothing greater would happen during Earth's 3rd millennium!

Well alright, so in the next chapter I'm going to show you the secret prophetic words God hid in Creation Day #4's narrative in order to prophesy the greatest event to take place during Earth's 4th millennium. This millennium would run from years 3,000 to 4,000. Do you see it already? You just learned Jesus DIED on the cross during Earth's 4,000 year! That means Jesus Christ lived his whole life during Earth's fourth millennium. So what do you think God prophesied about in Day 4 of Creation? I think you know!

CHAPTER 7

Creation Day 4
John the Baptist & Jesus Christ

Remember, each (24 hour) Creation day foretold of a future 1,000 year period, and in each day God hid words prophesying the greatest event He had planned to occur in that day's future millennium. So we've reached Creation Day #4 now, which foretold of Earth's 4th millennium, running from years 3,000 to 4,000. What did God prophesy in this day's events about this future millennium? He foretold the coming of the forerunner (John the Baptist) and the Messiah (Christ Jesus). That's right, in Day 4 of Creation God prophesied of John the Baptist and Jesus, which foretold their ENTIRE earthly lives would be lived during Earth's 4th millennium. In other words, both of them would live and die sometime between Earth's 3,000th to 4,000th years!

So let's look at the Creation narrative first, and I'll tell you how God did this. And then I'm going to prove to you (from the Bible) that John the Baptist & Jesus lived and died during Earth's 4th millennium. So Day 4's Creation narrative reads like this ...

And God said, Let there be lights in the firmament of the heaven to divide the day from the night; and let them be for signs, and for seasons, and for days, and years:

And let them be for lights in the firmament of the heaven to give light upon the earth: and it was so.

And <u>God made two great lights</u>; <u>the greater light to rule the day, and the lesser light to rule the night</u>: he made the stars also.

And God set them in the firmament of the heaven to give light upon the earth,

And to rule over the day and over the night, and to divide the light from the darkness: and God saw that it was good.

And the evening and the morning were the <u>FOURTH</u> day. (Genesis 1:14-19)

So where's the hidden prophecy? It's the line "God made two great lights; the GREATER LIGHT to rule the day (which was the sun), and the LESSER LIGHT to rule the night (which was the moon)" (Genesis 1:16). Friend, these words foretold of Jesus & John the Baptist, for later in His Word God would define (characterize) Jesus as the greater light (like the sun) and John the Baptist as the lesser light (like the moon).

Listen to how the Holy Spirit led the Apostle John to compare John the Baptist & Jesus: "There was a man sent from God, whose name was John (this is John the Baptist). The same came for a witness, to bear witness of the Light ... He was not that Light, but was sent to bear witness of that Light. That was the true Light (this is talking about Jesus now) which lighteth every man that cometh into the world. He was in the world, and the world was made by him, and the world knew him not." (John 1:6-10).

Do you see here the Apostle John is referring to both John the Baptist & Jesus as lights? He calls Jesus the true light, as Jesus himself said, "I am the light of the world" (John 8:12). And he refers to John the Baptist as a light in the fact that he "bears witness" to Jesus' light. Well, do you realize this is the exact same relationship between the moon and the sun in our physical world? The moon is not a true light source; it doesn't create its own light. But the sun does; it's a true light source. So the moon is a light source ONLY in the fact that it bears witness to the sun's light! Literally, it reflects the sun's light. Therefore, the moon is a light, but it's a lesser light than the sun. And this is exactly the relationship the Holy Spirit led the Apostle John to write about John the Baptist & Jesus ... John the Baptist was not that light, but he was sent to bear witness of that Light. That light, the true light, was Jesus.

So God was confirming here that John the Baptist was the lesser light (like the moon) and Jesus is the greater light (like the sun). And in fact, we even have a Scripture verse referring to Jesus as the sun, the S-U-N. Malachi wrote: "But unto you that fear my name shall the Sun of righteousness arise with healing in his wings" (Malachi 4:2). Isn't that amazing? The "sun of righteousness" in this verse is clearly talking about Jesus!

But here's what's even more amazing ... twice in the Gospels God actually used the adjectives "greater" and "lesser" when referring to Jesus & John the Baptist, respectively. This is mind-blowing! Listen, there's very little recorded in the Bible of the things John the Baptist said, and yet this is one of them: "He (Jesus) must become greater and I must become less" (John 3:30). Are you kidding me? Friend, John was talking about Jesus here! Jesus must become greater and John the Baptist must become less! The greater and lesser lights! Isn't that amazing? The Holy Spirit led John the Baptist to speak those words! Why? Because God wanted them recorded in the Bible to confirm fulfillment of his Creation Day 4 prophecy – the greater & lesser lights had arrived on the world scene.

Then we have these words from Jesus about John the Baptist: "He (John the Baptist) was a burning and a shining light: and ye were willing for a season to rejoice in his light. But I have a GREATER witness than John's; for the works which the Father has given Me to finish – the very works that I do – bear witness of Me, that the Father has sent Me" (John 5:35-36). Wow! Do you see it again? This time God directly calls John the Baptist a light, but then He says Jesus' light (or witness) is greater than John's. Mind blowing! The greater and lesser lights! So John 1:6-10; John 3:30, and John 5:35-36 are literally the fulfillment verses for what God had prophesied to happen in Genesis 1:16 [See Figure 8]. I am telling you the truth … God prophesied the coming of John the Baptist & Jesus Christ in Day 4 of Creation.

So let me explain to you now how God proved John the Baptist & Jesus lived their lives during Earth's fourth 1,000 year period, in perfect fulfillment of His Creation Day 4 prophecy. As we know, Earth's fourth

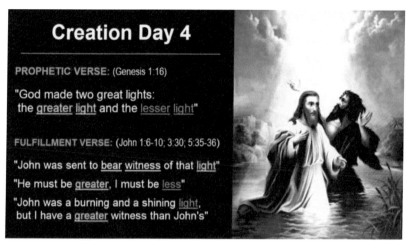

Creation Day 4

PROPHETIC VERSE: (Genesis 1:16)

"God made two great lights:
the greater light and the lesser light"

FULFILLMENT VERSE: (John 1:6-10; 3:30; 5:35-36)

"John was sent to bear witness of that light"
"He must be greater, I must be less"
"John was a burning and a shining light,
but I have a greater witness than John's"

Figure 8 – Creation Day 4 Prophecy

millennium ends with year 4,000, so this is what God did … He prophesied the Messiah (Jesus Christ) would DIE (on the cross) during Earth's 4,000 year! He actually prophesied this fact 10 times in the Bible, and we're going look at 6 of them shortly. Next, God recorded that Jesus ascended back into heaven 40 days after his resurrection (Acts 1:3), and since his resurrection was only 3 days after his death, then it was only 43 days after his death when Christ left planet Earth. So this proved it was still Earth's 4,000th year when Jesus left Earth. In other words, God left no doubt about it in His Word that Jesus lived his entire (approximately 33 year life) all during the final years of Earth's 4th millennium. He lived from roughly year 3,967 to the year 4,000, and then he was gone! And then to prove to us that John the Baptist did the same, in the Bible God recorded the birth of John the Baptist (within a year of Christ's birth) and then He recorded the shocking story of his death (his beheading) BEFORE Jesus' death. So it was that simple! John the

Baptist & Jesus (the lesser & greater lights) lived and died all during Earth's 4th millennium, in perfect fulfillment of God's Creation Day 4 prophecy! Amazing!

So let's take a look now at 6 times God prophesied the Messiah (Christ Jesus) would die for us during Earth's 4,000th year. I'll list them first, and then we'll talk briefly about each one. And when we're done, you're going to see there's NO denying that Jesus Christ was hanging on a cross in Jerusalem the very year planet Earth was making its 4,000th trip around the sun from Creation. So here we go ...

1) The Killing of the Egyptian Taskmaster
2) The Passover Lamb Requirements
3) The Red Sea Deliverance Event
4) The Story of Samson
5) The Dimensions of the Temple Altar
6) The Resurrection of Lazarus from the Dead

Alright, so on #1 (The Killing of the Egyptian Taskmaster) ... this is the story of Moses again, and we talked all about God's parabolic message behind this story in chapter 6 of this book. If you remember, Moses represented Jesus. He was sent by God to destroy Egypt's power over the Israelites, foreshadowing how Jesus would destroy Satan's power over us. But what I didn't tell you about was that God actually played out a mini-prophetic picture of this (before the Red Sea event) in an incident of Moses killing an Egyptian taskmaster.

The story goes like this: "And when Moses was a full **40** years old, it came into his heart to visit his brethren the children of Israel. And seeing one of them suffer wrong, he defended him, and avenged him that was oppressed, and smote the Egyptian" (Acts 7:23-24). Friend, do you see Moses' age when this happened? He was 40 years old! Now come on … you know as well as me he could have been anything … 32 years old, 38, 44, or whatever. In fact, Moses' age didn't even need to be recorded for this event. I mean who cares, right? But no, friend, God was prophesying! God wanted Moses to destroy an Egyptian taskmaster's power over an Israelite when he was precisely 40 years old, because this foretold Jesus would destroy Satan's power over us when Earth was precisely 4,000 years old! Wow!

So on #2 (The Passover Lamb Requirements) … this is also part of the story of Moses. God sent 10 plagues on the kingdom of Egypt to force Pharaoh to free the Israelites, and the 10th plague was the death plague. To escape death God commanded the Israelites to kill a Passover Lamb and spread its blood on their doorposts. When the angel of death saw the blood, he would pass over that house and not kill anyone inside. Now listen, this whole "Passover Lamb" scenario was also conceived by God to prophesy about the coming Messiah (Christ Jesus). It was Jesus who would be the sacrificial Passover Lamb of God. So God gave the Israelites 8 specific requirements to keep in regard to their Passover Lamb, and they were ALL further prophecies about Jesus! In other words, when Jesus arrived on the world scene, he literally fulfilled all 8 requirements God had given the Israelites to keep in regard to their Passover Lamb!

And you can learn about these in the Moses chapter of my book "*Undeniable Biblical Proof Jesus Christ Will*

Return to Planet Earth Exactly 2,000 Years After the Year of His Death", but for now I just want to focus on two of the requirements. God commanded the Israelites: "In the **10**th day of this month they shall take to them every man a lamb ... and ye shall keep it up until the **14**th day of the same month: and the whole assembly of the congregation of Israel shall kill it in the evening" (Exodus 12:3-6). So it was to be a **FOUR** day period from when they would "choose" their lamb to when they would "sacrifice" it? Do you understand what this means? These 4 days mirrored the first 4 days in the Creation story, prophetically representing 4,000 years of time! In other words, it would be 4 days (4,000 years) from when Christ was chosen as our Messiah to when he would be sacrificed. Peter informed us: "You were redeemed ... with the precious blood of Christ, a lamb without blemish or defect. He was chosen BEFORE THE CREATION of the world" (I Peter 1:18-20). Wow, so carefully hidden in God's requirements for the Israelite's choosing day and killing day of the Passover Lamb God prophesied it would be a 4 day period (meaning 4,000 years!) from when the Lamb of God was chosen (before the creation of the world) to when he was sacrificed (on the cross)! Glory to God!

Alright, so #3 (The Red Sea Deliverance Event) ... this is everything we discussed last time in chapter 6. We learned God delivered the Israelites at the Red Sea (through Moses' outstretched arms) after they had been in bondage for **400** years. In this way, God was foretelling, yet again, that Jesus would deliver us from our bondage by dying on a cross (with outstretched arms) after we'd been in bondage for 4,000 years. So again, Jesus died Earth's 4,000 year! Reread chapter 6 in this book to learn God's fascinating message behind that story. No preacher should be without this truth!

Ok, so on #4 (The Story of Samson) ... This story is just like the story of Moses, it's a real-life prophetic parable about Christ's 1st Coming. Samson was born to deliver the Israelites out of bondage to the Philistines. So Samson's life would be another man's God would use to prophesy of Jesus. His birth was supernatural, he was betrayed for money, and in his final scene of deliverance he stood with arms outstretched between two support pillars in the Philistine's temple, with all the Philistine rulers there, and calling on God for strength one last time, Samson cried, "Let me die with the Philistines!" He then pushed over the pillars and the building collapsed. And as Samson died in the rubble, thousands of Philistines rulers died also, freeing the Israelites from their enemy. This whole event prophetically pictured our deliverer, Jesus, stretching out his arms on a cross and dying for us, freeing us from our enemy, Satan!

But here's the prophetic timing detail in the story of Samson: "And the children of Israel did evil again in the sight of the Lord; and the Lord delivered them into the hand of the Philistines **40** years" (Judges 13:1). Wow! There it is again! Friend, God raised up Samson to deliver the Israelites after they had been in bondage for 40 years. This was to prophesy, yet again, that God would raise up Jesus to deliver us after we'd been in bondage for 4,000 years! In other words, yet again, Christ DIED for us (on the cross) during Earth's 4,000 year. Are you starting to see how all these stories in the Bible, all their little numbers and happenings are actually prophetic! Isn't the Bible amazing?

Ok, so #5 (The Dimensions of the Temple Altar) ... this is simple. God gave Solomon the dimensions for building the Temple altar, which was the place where all the lambs would be sacrificed, all of them pointing to Jesus who would be the TRUE sacrificial Lamb of God. So here's the dimensions: "Solomon made a bronze altar 20 cubits long, 20 cubits wide and 10 cubits high" (II Chronicles 4:1). Multiplying these 3 numbers together (length x width x height) and we get the volume (or the fullness) of the Temple altar. So what's 20 x 20 x 10 equal? **<u>4,000</u>** cubic cubits!!! God wanted the Temple altar's volume (or fullness) to be 4,000 cubic cubits! Why? Because this foretold the "fullness of time" when the Messiah (the true Lamb of God) would be sacrificed for us would be Earth's 4,000th year! Paul wrote: "When the <u>fullness</u> of the time was come, God sent forth his Son Jesus" (Galatians 4:4). Wow! This "fullness of time" was foretold in the Temple Altar's "fullness of size" – 4,000 years!!!

Ok, so on #6 (The Resurrection of Lazarus from the Dead) ... this is the story where Jesus raised a dead man (Lazarus) back to life. This miracle was performed by Jesus only weeks before his death. This means it was already Earth's 4,000th year! Planet Earth was already making its 4,000th trip around the sun (counted from Creation) when this miracle happened. But are you ready for this ... this story is also prophesy! God controlled this story (just weeks before Christ's death on the cross!) to prophesy one more time (one last time!) that Jesus would die for mankind during Earth's 4,000 year!

Asking for the stone to be rolled away, Martha informed Jesus how long Lazarus had been dead: "Lord, by this time there is a stench (he stinks): for he has been dead **FOUR** days" (John 11:39). Wow! There it is again! The first 4 Creation days! In raising Lazarus back to life, after him being dead for 4 days, God was prophesying, "Mankind's souls would be <u>dead</u> to sin for 4 days (or 4,000 years) until the Messiah would die for them on the cross, giving them life again! Absolutely mind-blowing! And just weeks later Jesus fulfilled the prophetic story of Lazarus, as well as all 6 of the prophecies I've just revealed to you, as he died on the cross for us!

So there you have it … there's 6 times in God's Word where He prophesied Jesus Christ would die on the cross during Earth's 4,000 solar year. Sometimes He used the number 4, sometimes 40, sometimes 400, and even 4,000 to prophesy this truth! It's truly amazing what God has done in His Word! But there's no denying the fact that Jesus Christ DIED for us (on the cross) during Earth's 4,000 year, and he left planet Earth that same year just 43 days later. So Jesus lived his entire earthly life during Earth's 4th millennium (years 3,967 - 4,000) in perfect fulfillment of the "Greater Light" being created in Day 4 of Creation.

And as for John the Baptist, the "Lesser Light", the story of his death is in Matthew chapter 14. And I'm not going to quote it here, but I'll tell you what Jesus did when he learned of John's beheading: "When Jesus heard what had happened, he withdrew by boat privately to a solitary place" (Matthew 14:13). Friend, there's the proof that John the Baptist died BEFORE Jesus died! In other words, God left no doubt about it ... John the Baptist also lived and died during Earth's 4th millennium in perfect fulfillment of the "Lesser Light" being created in Day 4 of Creation. Absolutely Amazing!

And to help you understand how remarkable this all is ... just realize we're told very little about the deaths of anyone in the New Testament, like Zechariah & Elizabeth, Mary & Joseph, Jesus' disciples, and on and on. So why would God record John the Baptist's death in the Bible! Why not let that be a mystery, like the deaths of all the others? Prophecy, my friend! Prophecy!!! God had prophecy to fulfill. The "Lesser Light" was created during day 4 of Creation, foretelling John the Baptist would live and die during Earth's 4th millennium. He could not live into the 5th millennium! And so John died a young man, because God needed him too! And we're told the story of his death, so we would all know ... God will always be faithful in fulfilling His Word!

Well I pray this has been a blessing to you. Learning the truth that Jesus DIED for us (on the cross) during Earth's 4,000th year (AD 28) allows us to know that Earth's 6,000th year (AD 2028) has not come yet! It let's us know God's (7 Day / 7,000 year) master plan is still in effect! Remember me telling you in chapter 3 how Bible prophecy teachers today have abandoned this truth? Somehow, they got it in their heads that Jesus was BORN year 4,000. But if this was so, it would mean he lived during Earth's 5th millennium (years 4,000 - 4,033). But do you see now, this is wrong!!! They don't know the truths in this book! They don't know God's creation of the "Greater Light" in day 4 of Creation foretold Jesus would live and die during Earth's 4th millennium. They just don't know!

So listen, if you have connections to any of these teachers, please send them this book. It's time they learn God's secret prophecies in the Bible. It's time we all get on the same page! If we could unite on a global front, we could hit the devil HARD with the prophetic truth of God's Word! I truly believe we'd have global revival if the information in this book got into the hands of every human being on Earth. But we've got to unite! As long as Satan has us all scattered, each saying our own thing, we will never accomplish much! So I'm asking you, humbly, if you know any of these teachers, please get them this information. We will be forever thankful.

Alright, so we have two more days left in the Creation story to talk about – days 5 & 6. So in the next chapter I'm going to reveal to you God's hidden words (secret prophecy) in Creation Day #5 concerning the greatest event He had planned to occur during Earth's 5th millennium, which ran from years 4,000 to 5,000. This one is deep, so you'll need to put on your thinking caps!

CHAPTER 8

Creation Day 5
Holy Spirit (Pentecost)

Remember now, in this book we're revealing the secret prophesies God hid in EACH Creation Day foretelling the greatest event He had planned to occur in that day's future millennium. Note: these aren't small meaningless events that were prophesied! No, rather these were hands down THE GREATEST EVENTS God had planned to occur in each millennium! That's what makes it so amazing! That's what makes it obviously true!

So to recap, in Day 1 of Creation God prophesied the Fall of Adam & Eve in the Garden of Eden (which took place during Earth's first 1,000 years, year 1). In Day 2 of Creation God prophesied the Global Flood of Noah's day (which happened during Earth's second 1,000 years, year 1,656). In Day 3 of Creation God prophesied the parting of the Red Sea (which took place during Earth's third 1,000 year period, year 2,638). And in Day 4 of Creation God prophesied the lives of John the Baptist & Jesus (and without a doubt they both lived and died during Earth's fourth 1,000 year period, leaving Earth year 4,000). So just think … God knew all these things were going to happen from the Creation of the world! Stunning! And God's Plan is still being carried out perfectly, just as He prophesied it would through Isaiah: "I declared the end from the beginning, and from long ago what is not yet done, saying: My plan will take place, for I will do all my will!" (Isaiah 46:10) Wow!

So here we are now at Creation Day #5, which prophesied of Earth's 5th millennium (running from years 4,000 to 5,000). This millennium was the beginning of the "Last Days" in God's 6 Day plan (or 6,000 year plan) before the End arrives at Christ's return. Think about it, the last 2 days of a 6 day plan are the LAST DAYS! Literally, they are the last 2 days! So when you see the term "Last Days" used in the Bible, understand it represents a 2,000 year period. It runs from the year of Christ' death (which was Earth's 4,000 year) to the year of his return (which will be Earth's 6,000 year). THAT two millennium period is the "Last Days" in God's eyes! And I'll show you a Scripture verse soon proving this fact. But just understand … we've been living in the "Last Days" for a long time now because this 2,000 year period will end Feast of Trumpets 2028!

So ok, in looking at Creation Day #5, what did God prophesy in this day's events concerning Earth's 5th millennium? He prophesied the outpouring of the Holy Ghost (Spirit) that would occur! Earth's 5th millennium was the start of a new and powerful outpouring of God's Holy Spirit on mankind. It would be Jesus who would send this Holy Ghost (the "comforter" as he called it) and it would arrive with fresh anointing and fresh truth. So let's read the Creation narrative first, and then I'll explain to you how God prophesied of it …

> And God said, <u>Let the waters bring forth abundantly the moving creature that hath life</u>, and fowl that may fly above the earth in the open firmament of heaven.
>
> And God created great whales, and every living creature that moveth, which the waters brought forth abundantly, after their kind, and every winged fowl after his kind: and God saw that it was good.
>
> And God blessed them, saying, Be fruitful, and multiply, and fill the waters in the seas, and let fowl multiply in the earth.
>
> And the evening and the morning were the <u>FIFTH</u> day. (Genesis 1:20-23)

So where's the prophesy? It's the line "Let the WATERS BRING FORTH ABUNDANTLY the moving CREATURE that HATH LIFE" (Genesis 1:20). Friend, these words foretold of the Holy Ghost (the Comforter) which would begin being poured out on the day of Pentecost just 10 days after Jesus left planet Earth.

So to understand how these words foretold of the Holy Ghost, we need to learn what God likened the Spirit too. Jesus said, "If anyone thirsts, let him come unto me, and drink. He that believes in me, as the Scripture has said, out of his belly shall flow rivers of living water. (But this he spoke concerning the Spirit, whom those believing on him would receive; for the Holy Ghost was not yet given, because Jesus was not yet glorified) (John 7:37-39). Ah, do you see, God likened the Holy Ghost (or the Holy Spirit) to water that gives life!

Well this is what the prophecy is saying in Day 5 of Creation "Let the waters bring forth abundantly the moving Creature that hath life." See the water is bringing forth life! But not only that ... it's bringing forth abundant life! Well Jesus made this connection too! He said: "I am come that they might have life, and that they might have it more abundantly" (John 10:10). Wow! Friend, it's the Holy Ghost that gives this abundant life. But not only that, notice in the Creation prophecy it's the "creature" that's receiving this life! Well listen to Jesus' command to his disciples: "Go into all the world and preach the gospel to every creature" (Mark 16:15). It's the exact same words! In the Creation story, it's the water that's bringing forth abundant life in the creature. And this is EXACTLY what the Holy Ghost does ... it brings forth abundant life in the creature (which is us). Literally, the Holy Ghost in us is the seal (or the guarantee) that we'll obtain eternal life in heaven one day, and that will be ABUNDANT life!

So John 7:37-39, John 10:10, and Mark 16:15 are literally the fulfillment verses for what God had prophesied to happen in Genesis 1:20 [See Figure 9]. I am telling you the truth ... God prophesied the coming of the Holy Ghost in Day 5 of Creation, and it became a reality, right on time, at the start of Earth's fifth millennium! And realize ... this wasn't just a one time fulfillment event. Sure, it happened first on the day of Pentecost, 10 days after Christ's ascension (which was Earth's 4,000 year), but you can read about it happening again and again in the book of Acts, which chronicled the next 35 years of Earth's history. So there's no doubt, God's Creation Day 5 prophecy of "the water giving abundant life to the creature" was continually being fulfilled during Earth's fifth millennium, which as I stated early was the start of the "Last Days" (or the Last 2 Days!) in God's 6 Day plan for planet Earth.

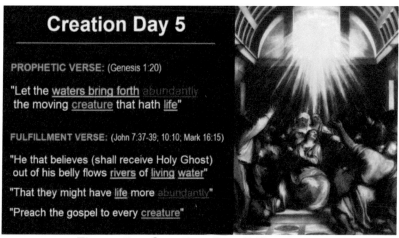

Figure 9 – Creation Day 5 Prophecy

Listen to what Peter stood up and said on the day of Pentecost (right after the Holy Ghost was poured out for the very first time and people began to speak in languages not their own). He said: "Fellow Jews, listen carefully to what I say. These people are not drunk, as you suppose. It's only nine in the morning! No, this is what was spoken by the prophet Joel: "And it shall come to pass in the LAST DAYS, saith God, that I will pour out my Spirit upon all flesh: and your sons and your daughters shall prophesy." (Acts 2:14-17). Wow! Did you see it? Peter was now calling it … the LAST DAYS! That's because it was now Earth's 4,000 year and the last 2 days (or the last 2,000 years) in God's 6,000 year plan for planet Earth had begun.

And these Last Two Days are very special in God's eyes. Why? Because they lead to the return of Jesus Christ! They lead to the time of Satan and his demons being locked up in the bottomless pit! They lead to the marriage Supper of the Lamb! They lead to Christ setting up his millennial Sabbath reign on Earth in fulfillment of Day 7 in the Creation story! And oh how glorious that time will be, no more wickedness, no more war, only peace and love for God's resurrected saints on Earth! So yeah, the last 2 Days (or 2,000 years) are VERY special in God's eyes. So special, that He prophesied of them many times in His Word. And I'm going to tell you about 5 of these prophecies right now, revealing to you how they verify the Last Days will be a 2,000 year period, running from the year of Christ's death (Earth's 4,000 solar year) to the year of his return (Earth's 6,000 solar year).

1) The 7 Day Creation Story
2) The Hosea Prophecy
3) Parable of the Good Samaritan
4) The Demoniac from Gadara
5) Jesus Appears at Sea of Tiberias

Alright, so on #1 (The 7 Day Creation Story) ... this is fascinating! Because not only did God prophesy the speciality of the "Last Days" and their 2,000 year length of time, but in so doing He actually foretold the Messiah would die for us during Earth's 4,000 year! Did you hear that? I'm telling you God prophesied the Messiah (Christ Jesus) would die for us Earth's 4,000 year in the Creation story!!! Isn't that mind-blowing?

Remember in chapter 7 of this book I revealed to you 6 times in the Bible where God prophesied Jesus would die for us during Earth's 4,000 solar year. Well this now is a seventh! But it was actually the very first time God prophesied this truth!

So here's what He did … Days 5 & 6 in the Creation story were the ONLY **TWO** DAYS when He created life, meaning those creatures with the "breath of life" in them. The fish of the sea and the birds of the air were created on Day 5, and jumping ahead, the beasts of the field and us (mankind) were created on Day 6. So Days 1 thru 4 in the Creation story contained NO LIFE. In this way, God secretly prophesied mankind would be DEAD to sin for 4 days (or 4,000 years) until the Messiah would die on the cross, giving us life! After that, mankind would live for 2 days (or 2,000 years) in the finished life-giving work of Christ. So that's why God made life ONLY on Day's 5 & 6 in the Creation story. So sit back sometime and meditate on the fact that from the Creation of the world God foretold the YEAR of the Messiah's death – Earth's 4,000 year! Wow!

Alright, so #2 (The Hosea Prophecy) … this is simple. This is a direct prophecy confirming what God had already declared in the Creation story – specifically, that from Christ's <u>death</u> to his <u>return</u> would be a Two Day period. Hosea wrote: "I will go and return to my place, till they acknowledge their offense, and seek my face: in their affliction they will seek me early … After **TWO** DAYS will he revive us: in the third day he will raise us up, and we shall live in his sight" (Hosea 5:15 - 6:2). Wow! Friend, this prophecy was written to the Jews, foretelling it would be a TWO DAY period from Christ's ascension (when he would "return to his place") until his Second Coming at the time of the Jew's "affliction" during the Antichrist's reign. After these 2 Days (or 2,000 years) begins the 3rd day (years 6,000 to 7,000) when "we shall live in his sight" during the beautiful Sabbath reign of Jesus Christ! So this is a straightforward prophecy, undeniably proclaiming the length of time between Christ's ascension and his return will be exactly 2 days (meaning 2,000 years).

Ok, so #3 (Parable of the Good Samaritan) … this is really cool. This is a parable Jesus spoke, and the early church knew its meaning. The parable goes like this: "A certain man went down from Jerusalem to Jericho, and fell among thieves, who stripped him of his clothing, wounded him, and departed, leaving him half dead … a certain Samaritan, as he journeyed, came where he was. And when he saw him, he had compassion. So he went to him and bandaged his wounds, pouring on oil and wine; and he set him on his own animal, brought him to an inn, and took care of him. On the next day, when HE DEPARTED, he took out **TWO** denarii, gave them to the innkeeper, and said to him, 'Take care of him; and whatever more you spend, when I COME AGAIN, I will repay you.' (Luke 10:30-35).

So here's the meaning of the parable: The certain man coming down out of Jerusalem represented Adam in the Garden of Eden. The thieves who stole from him and left him half-dead represented Satan. Remember, when Adam sinned in the Garden of Eden he experienced the first death. The second death awaits all who will NOT repent. So in other words, Satan (the "thief" who comes to kill) left Adam half dead. And understand, everything that's happening to Adam in this parable is applicable to ALL of us.

So then along comes the Good Samaritan, who represents Jesus. The Good Samaritan has compassion on the half-dead man, and does all he can to save him. This represents Jesus dying on the cross for us, giving us a chance at life again. But then the Good Samaritan hands the innkeeper two denarii and departs, saying "Take care of him, and WHEN I COME AGAIN, I'll repay you". Do you see it? This foretold Jesus would leave, but then he'd come back again!

So where's the timing prophecy in the parable. It's hidden in the TWO denarii Jesus gave the innkeeper! In Christ's day, ONE denarii represented an average man's wage for ONE Day's work. Jesus even told a parable in Matthew chapter 20 confirming this truth. It's the parable of the workers in the Vineyard. And if you read it, you'll see all the workers were paid one denarii for one day's work. So by the Good Samaritan giving the innkeeper TWO denarius, he was indirectly saying, "I'm coming back in TWO DAYS!" Wow! So the parable was prophesying, "Jesus Christ will return in 2 days (or 2,000 years) from the year he left!" Incredible! By the way, we made a video further explaining the Good Samaritan parable, and you can watch it by visiting our www.2028End.com website, clicking the "confirmations" link, and then visiting the "Parable of the Good Samaritan" page. I promise, it'll be a blessing!

Ok, so onto #4 (The Demoniac from Gadara) … this is amazing too! This is the story where Jesus casts out a legion of demons from a wild man living in the caves, and the demons flee into a herd of pigs. The story is told in Matthew chapter 8, Mark chapter 5, and Luke chapter 8. And if you read all 3 accounts, you'll get the full truth of the story. In Matthew were told the demons cried out to Jesus, "What do you want with us, Son of God? Have you come here to torment us BEFORE the TIME?" (Matthew 8:29). Wow! Friend, these words are the clue to God's message behind this miracle. Most people don't realize this ... but Jesus' miracles contained messages! Jesus even said this after the feeding of the 5,000: "You are looking for me because you ate the bread and had all you wanted, NOT because you understood my miracles!" (John 6:26). Wow!

If you remember in chapter 7 of this book, I told you God's secret message behind Jesus' miracle of raising Lazarus from the dead: Lazarus was dead for 4 days before being raised back to life. This prophesied mankind would be dead to sin for 4 days (or 4,000 years) until Christ would give us life again by dying on a cross. See it wasn't just a miracle! The miracle contained a message!

And such is the case with the demoniac from Gadara story. Jesus cast the demons out of the man, miraculously, and they went into a large herd of pigs that were grazing on a nearby hillside. This is what the Bible records: "And the unclean spirits went out and entered into the pigs, and that herd ran to a precipice (or a cliff) and fell into the sea below, about **2,000** of them, and they drowned in the water" (Mark 5:13).

Friend, this scene was a visual representation of what's going to happen in the spirit realm during Christ's return Earth's 6,000 year. At that time, the demons are going to be thrown into the bottomless pit! This is the TIME their torment begins! But check this out … God labeled "pigs" unclean in the Old Testament. The Israelites were never to eat them. So do you see, watching pigs (or unclean animals) fall over a cliff to their doom below, was literally like watching the demons (or unclean spirits) fall to their doom in the bottomless pit at the time of Christ's return? Amazing, right!

But where's the timing prophecy? Friend, it's hidden in the number of pigs that perished! The story records … there were about 2,000 pigs! Now why would this number be included? Who cares? Why not just say "a large herd of pigs". Because God was prophesying! And these 2,000 pigs represented 2,000 years of time! Now were there exactly 2,000 pigs? I don't know. I doubt anyone counted them. Although I wouldn't be surprised if there were! But either way, God wanted this number "2,000" attached to this story, because it foretold WHEN the demons TIME of torment would arrive, which was the subject they alluded to in their initial question to Jesus, "Have you come here to torment us, before the TIME?" And just realize one last thing about this story … it was already Earth's 4,000 year when this miracle happened, too. So the pigs were falling over the cliff to their doom during Earth's 4,000 year, and therefore the miracle was accurately prophesying Christ's return 2,000 years later – Earth's 6,000 year. Absolutely amazing!

So onto #5 (Jesus Appears at the Sea of Tiberias) ... this is really awesome too! After Christ's resurrection, one night seven of his disciples went fishing. They didn't catch anything, but in the morning (while they were still out on the boat) a voice from shore called out to them, "Throw your net on the right side of the boat and you'll catch some." So they did, and their net miraculously became full of fish! That's when John said to Peter, "It's the Lord". So Peter jumped in the water and headed to shore, and the rest hurried inland with the boat and the net full of fish. But when they got there, the Bible strangely records this: "When they landed, they saw a fire of burning coals there with fish on it, and some bread".

So Jesus already had a meal waiting for them? What's this about? Friend, the meal Jesus had prepared for his disciples represented the marriage supper of the Lamb! You can read about this banquet in Revelation chapter 19, but it was also prophesied by Isaiah in the Old Testament: "On this mountain the Lord Almighty will prepare a feast of rich food ... he will swallow up death forever. The sovereign Lord will wipe away the tears from all faces" (Isaiah 25:6-8). So when's this going to happen? Earth's 6,000 year, right after Christ's return! Jesus will prepare the marriage super of the Lamb for his saints, just like he had prepared the meal in this story for his disciples!

So where's the prophetic timing detail in the story? It's in this seemingly small detail: "But the other disciples (minus Peter) came in the little boat (for they were not far from the land, but about **200** cubits away), dragging the net full of fish" (John 21:8). Do you see it? When Jesus called out to them from the shore, the disciples were 200 cubits away from him!!! These 200 cubits represented the 2,000 years they were away from seeing him at the marriage supper of the Lamb! Wow! Realize this miracle also took place Earth's 4,000 year (it was after Christ's death and resurrection), and thus it too perfectly prophesied Jesus would return 2,000 years later – Earth's 6,000 year!

So there you have it … there's 5 times in God's Word where He prophesied the "Last Days" would be a 2 Day period (meaning a 2,000 year period) between the year of Christ's death (year 4,000) and the year of his return (year 6,000). He used the numbers 2, 200, and even 2,000 to proclaim this truth. He used the number "20" also, but I don't have time to get into all that. But if you study the number "20" in God's Word, you'll see it's His number for "redemption". That's because God knew from the Creation of the World that mankind would live for 2,000 years in the finished redemption work of the Messiah until their final redemption draws nigh at his return. So really, God used the numbers 2, 20, 200, and even 2,000 to prophesy of the "Last Days", just like He used the numbers 4, 40, 400, and 4,000 to prophesy Christ's death Earth's 4,000 year. It's truly remarkable what God has done in His Word!

What's even further fascinating to me is God attached this redemption number 20 to my book *"Undeniable Biblical Proof Jesus Christ Will Return to Planet Earth Exactly 2,000 Years After the Year of His Death"*. I received this prophetic 7 Day Creation message from God AND wrote the book (both) in the year 2008, which was 20 years from the end. It was literally Earth's 5,980th year when I was writing the book! So it was God's plan to unveil this incredible prophetic message to mankind just 20 years from the end. My book has 20 chapters. And miraculously, when I printed 5,000 copies of the book, they arrived packaged <u>20</u> books to a box with a shipping weight of 28 lbs! That's 20-28!!!

Friend, I'll never forget the night God gave me the title to the book back in 2008, showing it to me written in the shape of a cross: "*Undeniable Biblical Proof Jesus Christ Will Return to Planet Earth Exactly 2,000 Years After the Year of His Death.*" Then ten years later (in 2018) someone informed me, "Do you know the title to your book contains 20 words, if you count "2,000" as "two thousand?". Oh my goodness!!! My mind was blown!!! No, I didn't know that! And in the book (on pages 106 & 200) I even reveal how God attached the number "20" in the Bible to the cross, and then I find out God used exactly 20 words for the title of my book, forming the cross on the cover!!! Absolutely amazing!

So just think ... the cover shows a cross (representing Earth's 4,000 year) and a burning earth behind it (representing Earth's 6,000 year), while 20 words make up the cross and speak the prophetic message "*Undeniable Biblical Proof Jesus Christ Will Return to Planet Earth Exactly 2,000 Years After the Year of His Death*". So the <u>words</u> themselves are prophesying Christ's return 2,000 years after his death, but the <u>number</u> of words (20) is doing the same! It's literally as if God spoke the prophecy twice! This is mind-blowing to me! Friend, I don't know how else to say it, God has stamped His signature (His approval) all over that book! If you ever wanted to know if a book came from God, you have it with that one! God wants you to read it! God's Word says, "My people perish for lack of knowledge" (Hosea 4:6), and I know without a shadow of a doubt that that book (written by the Holy Spirit) contains the knowledge that could help save them, if they would only hear (read) it and apply it.

Well alright, so now you know what God prophesied in Day 5 of Creation concerning Earth's fifth millennium. It was all about the fresh anointing of the Holy Ghost that would arrive, the "water of life" giving abundant life to the creature. So in the next chapter were going to talk about Day 6 in the Creation story, which foretold of Earth's sixth millennium, running from years 5,000 to 6,000. This is the millennium that will end with the return of Jesus Christ; and we're inside the final decade of this age right now! So I'm going to reveal to you what God prophesied about this 6th millennium (something that has not yet happened!) and I'm going to reveal to you how we know Earth's 6,000 year will be the year AD 2028. So keep reading!

CHAPTER 9

Creation Day 6
Antichrist & Mark of Beast

Day #6 in the Creation week foretold of Earth's sixth 1,000 year period, running from years 5,000 to 6,000. And just like God hid a prophesy in each of the first 5 Creation Days foretelling the Greatest Event to take place in their respective future millenniums, so too God hid a secret prophesy in Creation Day 6 foretelling the greatest event to take place during Earth's 6th millennium. And that event was the coming of the Antichrist & the Great Tribulation period! So let's read the Creation narrative first, and then I'll tell you how God did this:

And God said, Let the earth bring forth the living creature after his kind, cattle, and creeping thing, and beast of the earth after his kind: and it was so.

And <u>God made the beast</u> of the earth after his kind, and cattle after their kind, and every thing that creepeth upon the earth after his kind: and God saw that it was good.

And God said, <u>Let us make man in our image</u>, after our likeness: and <u>let them have dominion over the fish of the</u>

sea, and over the fowl of the air, and over the cattle, and over all the earth, and over every creeping thing that creepeth upon the earth.

So God created man in his own image … male and female created he them.

And God blessed them, and God said unto them, Be fruitful, and multiply, and replenish the earth, and subdue it: and have dominion over every living thing that moveth upon the earth.

And God saw every thing that he had made, and, behold, it was very good. And the evening and the morning were the SIXTH day. (Genesis 1:24-31)

Ok, so where in all of this is the prophecy? It's in several places. It's the line "God made the BEAST" (Genesis 1:25). It's these lines "God said, Let us make man in our IMAGE, after our likeness (Genesis 1:26) … So God created man in his own IMAGE" (Genesis 1:27). It's also these lines "Let them have DOMINION over the fish of the sea, and over the fowl of the air, and over the cattle, and over all the earth (Genesis 1:26) … SUBDUE it: and have DOMINION over every living thing that moveth upon the earth" (Genesis 1:28). Friend, all these lines foretold of the Antichrist and his Great Tribulation period. How you ask? Because in God's Word the Antichrist is described as a beast, who will be a man, that will take dominion over all the Earth!

Fifteen times in Revelation chapter 13 the Antichrist is called a beast: "And they worshipped the beast, saying, Who is like unto the beast? Who is able to make war with him?" (Revelation 13:4). But at the same time the Bible reveals the Antichrist will be a man: "Let him that hath understanding count the number of the beast: for it is the number of a MAN; and his number is six hundred sixty-six" (Revelation 13:18). The Bible says this man will take dominion over all the Earth: "And it was given unto him to make war with the saints, and to overcome them: and power was given him over all kindreds, and tongues, and nations" (Revelation 13:7). Wow!

So do you see? The Antichrist will be a man, like unto a beast, who will rule over every living thing that moves upon the earth. And friend, this is EXACTLY what God prophesied in Day 6 of Creation … God made the beast, and then He made man, and he commanded the man to take rule over every living thing that moves upon the earth! There's also prophecy in the word "image" being used in Day 6 of Creation. It says "God created man in his own image" giving him life; well so too the Antichrist will proclaim that "HE is God" and he will create a man in HIS own image (called the image of the beast) and he will give it life: "And he had power to give life unto the image of the beast, that the image of the beast should speak" (Revelation 13:15). Wow! So even the words "God created man in his own image" were prophecy about the "image of the beast" the Antichrist would create! So it's perfectly clear … God prophesied the coming of the Antichrist in Day 6 of Creation, which foretold he would live during Earth's 6th millennium (meaning sometime between the years 5,000 to 6,000).

Thankfully the Bible tells us exactly WHEN he will reign and for how long! It says he will be given the last 42 months (3.5 years) right before Jesus Christ returns, which will occur Earth's 6,000 year: "And there was given unto him a mouth speaking great things and blasphemies; and power was given unto him to continue forty and two months" (Revelation 13:5). After this, Jesus will DESTROY the Antichrist during his return Feast of Trumpets 2028: "Then that lawless one (the Antichrist) will be revealed whom the Lord will bring to an End by the appearance of His coming" (II Thessalonians 2:8). So the Bible is clear … the Antichrist's dominion will be a 3.5 year period occurring during Earth's 5,997th to 6,000th year. THIS will be the TIME of the Great Tribulation, which corresponds to the years AD 2025 to AD 2028 on our calendar. So the Antichrist will reign the last 42 months (3.5 years) of Earth's 6th millennium in PERFECT fulfillment of God's Creation Day 6 prophecy!

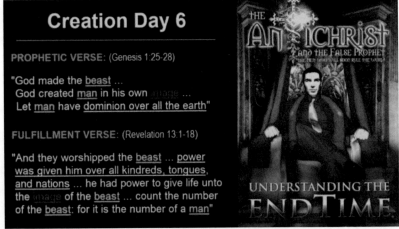

Figure 10 – Creation Day 6 Prophecy

So Revelation 13:4,7,18 are literally the (soon-to-be-fulfilled) fulfillment verses for what God prophesied to happen in Genesis 1:25-28 [See Figure 10]. Try and wrap your mind around this truth: there's still prophecy in the VERY FIRST CHAPTER of the Bible (Genesis chapter 1) that has NOT yet been fulfilled! It will be fulfilled in the next 10 years! Isn't that astounding? So much for those who say, "The Old Testament is over and done with!" No! Friend, the Bible is full of prophecy from its first page to its last! It's all alive and well! Truly, the testimony of Jesus is the spirit of prophecy!

Well ok, so now I want to reveal to you the times in God's Word where He prophesied the "End" will come Earth's 6,000 year. And since we know the Antichrist reigns the 3.5 years right before the End, these will prove the Antichrist's time will be during Earth's 6th millennium. I'll list them first, and then we'll talk briefly about each one.

1) The 7 Day Creation Story
2) The Story of Noah
3) The Job Prophecy
4) Nebuchadnezzar's Golden Image
5) Jesus on the Mount of Transfiguration

Alright, so on #1 (The 7 Day Creation Story) … we discussed this one in chapter 3 of this book. "God Declared the End from the Beginning" by literally using the word "End" in the Creation story: "And on the seventh day God ENDED his work which he had made, and he rested on the seventh day" (Genesis 2:2). These words were prophesying that after **SIX** days (meaning 6,000 years) God will make an End to His creation! How will He do this? By burning the entire surface of planet Earth with fire during Christ's return: "The Lord Jesus shall be revealed from heaven with his mighty angels, in FLAMING FIRE taking vengeance on them that know not God" (II Thessalonians 1:7-8).

Friend, THIS is the day the rapture (gathering) occurs! In fact, it's the ONLY REASON there's a "catching away" needed! It's so God's people don't get burned up in the fire! The fire is the wrath of God! And God's people (those alive and remaining) are NOT appointed to that wrath! So God declared this "End" would come Earth's 6,000 year by saying He "made an end to His Creation" after 6 Days in the Creation story! THAT'S how God declared the end from the beginning!

Alright, so #2 (The Story of Noah) ... we discussed this one in chapter 5 of this book. Noah was **600** years old when the entire surface of planet Earth was destroyed with a flood of water. This prophesied planet Earth will be 6,000 years old when its entire surface will be destroyed with a flood of fire! And during the Flood, Noah's righteous family was "caught up" into the air to safety (in the Ark) as a world of ungodly people perished below. This whole scene was a prophetic picture of Christ's return Earth's 6,000 year; for on that day Christ's righteous family will be "caught up" into the air to safety (in the clouds) as a world of ungodly beast-marked people perish below. Reread chapter 5 in this book to learn all about God's truth behind the story of Noah.

Ok, so on #3 (The Job Prophecy) ... this is simple. This is a straightforward prophecy proclaiming the End will arrive after 6 periods! Job wrote: "He shall deliver thee in **SIX** troubles: yea, in seven there shall no evil touch thee" (Job 5:19). Wow! Friend, these words were reinforcing what God had already prophesied through the 7 Day Creation story: mankind will live through 6 millenniums of trouble (where Satan roams free seeking whom he may devour) but in the 7th millennium (which will be the Sabbath reign of Christ) no evil will touch mankind, because Satan will be locked up in the bottomless pit. So there it is again – the End will come after 6 troubles, meaning 6,000 years!

Ok, so #4 (Nebuchadnezzar's Golden Image) ... this is fascinating. Around 600 BC Nebuchadnezzar was the mighty king of Babylon, and he ruled the world at that time. And one night he had a dream of a huge metallic statue (that from the head to the feet) represented Earth's world kingdoms right up till the time of Christ's return. The prophet Daniel told him, "Nebuchadnezzar, your kingdom, the kingdom of Babylon, is represented by the head of gold on the statue."

Well inspired by the dream and his ego, Nebuchadnezzar decided to have a massive statue built (in his IMAGE) ... made completely of gold. And then he commanded everyone: "O people, nations, and languages ... fall down and worship the golden IMAGE that Nebuchadnezzar the king hath set up" (Daniel 3:4-5). Do you understand the story? Friend, this is another real-life prophetic parable, just like the stories of Noah & Moses! But in this story, God was playing out a prophetic picture of the coming Antichrist (and what he would do!) hundreds of years before Revelation chapter 13 was ever written! So Nebuchadnezzar represents the Antichrist, and the image he set up of himself to be worshipped represents the image the Antichrist will setup of himself to be worshipped in the soon-to-be rebuilt Temple in Jerusalem.

Well, long story short, three men (Shadrach, Meshach, & Abednego) would NOT worship Nebuchadnezzar's image. So they were thrown into a furnace of FIRE to be burned alive! But they didn't die! Jesus appeared with them in the fire, and they were not harmed. So they came out of the fire, and the ones who had thrown them into the fire were now thrown into the fire. And Guess what happened? They perished! These were the men who had served Nebuchadnezzar, who had worshipped his image!

So here's God's prophetic message behind the story: Those who worship the Antichrist and his image (those who take his mark!) will perish in the fire during Christ's return! But those who will NOT worship the Antichrist or his image (those who will NOT take his mark!) will be delivered from the fire that blankets planet Earth on the day of Christ's return. They will be "caught up" into the air to safety, where Jesus will appear with them in the clouds! So in this story, Shadrach, Meshach, & Abednego represented the raptured saints on the day of Christ's return Earth's 6,000 year!

So where's the prophetic timing detail in the story? It's hidden in the height of the statue Nebuchadnezzar built. Remember, this statue was inspired by the dream Nebuchadnezzar had, which represented ALL of Earth's world kingdoms (from the head to the feet) until the time of Christ's return. So how much time did mankind have until the end? The Bible records: "Nebuchadnezzar the king made an image of gold, whose height was **60** cubits ... and he set it up in the plain of Dura, in the province of Babylon" (Daniel 3:1). Wow! Friend, these 60 cubits represented the 6,000 years mankind had to rule himself until Christ would set up HIS millennial Sabbath Kingdom, which would have no end!

There's one last thing I want to mention about Nebuchadnezzar's story, because it further confirms the words God used in Day 6 of Creation really are prophecy about the coming Antichrist. Daniel told Nebuchadnezzar: "Thou, O King, are a king of kings: for the God of heaven hath given thee a kingdom, power, and strength, and glory. And wherever the children of men dwell, the beasts of the field and the fowls of the heaven hath he given into thine hand, and hath made thee ruler over them all." (Daniel 2:37-38). Wow! Friend, do you see these words are a throwback to God's words in Creation Day 6? Remember, I told you the words "Let man have dominion over the beast of the field, the fish of the sea, and the fowls of the air" were about the Antichrist? Well here they are written about Nebuchadnezzar, who was a prophetic picture of the coming Antichrist! So by saying these things about Nebuchadnezzar, God was confirming his words in Creation Day 6 REALLY WERE prophecy about the future Antichrist! I mean think about it sometime ... why would God want to say Nebuchadnezzar had rule over the beasts of the field and the birds of the air? Sounds ridiculous right? But not when you realize God wanted to confirm the truth of His prophetic words in Creation Day 6! Fascinating!

Ok, so #5 (Jesus on the Mount of Transfiguration) ... this is awesome too! One time Jesus declared to his disciples: "Truly I say unto you, some who are standing here shall not taste of death before they see the son of Man coming in his kingdom" (Matthew 16:28). The very next verse then says this: "Jesus took with him Peter, James, and John his brother, and led them up a high mountain by themselves. There He was transfigured before them. His face shone like the sun, and His clothes became as white as the light" (Matthew 17:1). Friend, this scene was the fulfillment of Christ's words in the previous verse! Jesus was talking about Peter, James and John! It was they who saw Christ transfigure into his glorified body, which is what he will look like when he returns! And when will this happen? The story records: "After **SIX** days, Jesus took with him Peter, James, and John ..." Wow! So there it is again – Jesus will return after 6 Days (meaning 6,000 years) to set up his Kingdom!

Well there you have it ... there's 5 times in God's Word where he prophesied the End will arrive Earth's 6,000 year. He used the numbers 6, 60, and even 600 to prophesy this truth. This was just like He used the set of numbers 4, 40, 400, and 4,000 to prophesy of Christ' death Earth's 4,000 year, and the set of numbers 2, 20, 200, and 2,000 to prophesy of the "Last Days" 2,000 year length of time between the year of Christ death and return. So God was very consistent with numbers when prophesying these truths in his Word!

Well alright, so now I want to reveal how we know Earth's 6,000 year will be the year AD 2028. How can we possibly know this? Friend, it's hidden in more Bible prophecy, along with an event that just happened in the past century! It all begins with Jesus' parable of the Fig Tree: "Now learn a parable of the fig tree; When its branch is yet tender, and puts forth leaves, you know that summer is near: So likewise, when you shall see all these things, know that my return is near, even at the doors. Truly I say unto you, THIS GENERATION shall not pass away, till all these things be fulfilled" (Matthew 24:32-34). What generation is Jesus talking about that will not all die before he returns?

The answer is in his parable! Remember in a parable things represent other things. And in God's Word the "fig tree" represents the nation of Israel. God said: "When I found Israel, it was like finding grapes in the desert; when I saw your ancestors, it was like seeing the first ripe figs on the FIG TREE" (Hosea 9:10). So in this parable, when Jesus says, "when you see the fig tree put forth leaves", he was prophesying "when you see the nation of Israel come back on the map!" It's THAT GENERATION of people who will not all pass away before my return! Well, friend, astonishingly this happened in 1948! Israel was declared a nation again May 14, 1948! The fig tree had put forth her leaves! And so the year 1948 began the final generation till Christ's return!

That leaves us with only one thing left to know ... how long is this generation Jesus was talking about? Is this information in the Bible? Yes! Psalms 90:10 says: "The days of our years are 70; and if by reason of strength they be **80** years, yet is their strength labour and sorrow; for it is SOON CUT OFF, and we FLY AWAY" (Psalms 90:10). So 80 years is the outside date for a generation! Well, if you add 80 years to 1948, what do you get? 2028!!! But that's not all. Notice this verse says the generation is "soon cut off and we fly away". What's that about? Friend, the words "soon cut off" and "we fly away" were God's way of linking this verse to Jesus' words in Matthew 24 (right before he told the parable of the Fig Tree). This was done to absolutely PROVE this verse holds the key to the length of the generation Jesus was talking about.

In Matthew 24, Jesus said: "For then shall be Great Tribulation, such as was not since the beginning of the world to this time, no, nor ever shall be. And except those days should be shortened, there should no flesh be saved: but for the elect's sake those days shall be shortened" (Matthew 24:21-22). In other words, the Great Tribulation period will be CUT OFF! The Antichrist's reign will be CUT OFF! How? By Christ's return! The Apostle John informed us in "The Revelation" the Antichrist's reign will only last 42 months, right up till Christ's return cuts his dominion short. See if Jesus wasn't returning, there's no telling how long the Antichrist would reign! 10 years, 20 years, 50 years, I don't know? But thankfully his time will be "soon cut off," and when it is ... the saints (alive and remaining) will "fly away" up into the air to meet Christ in the clouds! This is what Psalms 90:10 is talking about! So 80 years after the Fig Tree put forth leaves (meaning Israel became a nation again) in 1948 the Antichrist's Great Tribulation period will be "cut off" and the saints will "fly away"! 80 onto 1948 equals 2028! Friend, Jesus is going to return to Earth Feast of Trumpets AD 2028.

It was this knowledge along with everything else in this seminar that led me to write in my book back in 2008: "Consequently, my spirit believes Jesus' 2nd

Coming will occur in the year AD 2028, which places his death in AD 28. And now you know how I calculated 3972 BC (AD 2028 – 6,000 years) as the year of Creation!" Well friend, now you know too! It comes from the fact that Israel became a nation again in 1948, and 80 years later (2028) the Antichrist's time will be "cut off" and we will "fly away".

And amazingly, ever since I've written the book "*Undeniable Biblical Proof Jesus Christ Will Return to Planet Earth Exactly 2,000 Years After the Year of His Death*" God has been miraculously confirming His son's return in the year AD 2028. Visit our sobering website www.2028End.com sometime and read through them on the "confirmations" link. You'll be shocked! In 2013 a man in the UK dreamed of numbers in the sun. He saw 21, 22, 23, and 24 appear one after the other in the sun, and then it got real dark, like a terrible storm was coming! He saw fallen lampposts and torn down high tension wires. And then the sun came back again and he saw a huge number 28 filling up the sun, growing bigger and bigger, while angels chanted in unison, "Jesus is coming! Jesus is coming! Jesus is coming! This man's name is Alfred, and he knew nothing of our ministry when he had this dream in March 13, 2013. He found us a year later and emailed us his story. Visit his "numbers in the sun" page on our website and watch the video at the top. I'm telling you, it's the REAL DEAL!

Then on Feb 5, 2017, God supernaturally controlled America's biggest football game of the year (Super Bowl 51) to proclaim Christ's return in the year 2028. What He did in that game is mind-boggling! I'm not going to go into it here, but visit the confirmation webpage and watch the video at the top. You'll be stunned at what happened!

And there are more confirmations on our site. They're even people who know nothing about our ministry who believe wholeheartedly that Jesus died in the year AD 28. They get this solely from the Biblical and historical record. So I encourage you to visit each and every one of the confirmation pages to see what God's been doing! There's even a page for the "Parable of the Fig Tree" where you can learn more about it. Watch the video at the top of that page. It's precious information. Friend, I am telling you the truth ... God has literally been going out of His way to shout to the world, "My Son Jesus Christ is going to return to planet Earth 2,000 years after the year of His Death – Feast of Trumpets AD 2028! SO GET READY!!!!!"

Well, there's only one last chapter to go in this book! And in it we're going to discuss God's prophetic messages behind His 7 Feasts. You're going to find out God's Feasts prophesied the TIME (during a calendar year) when the Messiah would complete his most important assignments. And once and for all, you're going to learn what the phrase "no man knows the day or hour" is REALLY about. So by all means ... keep reading!

CHAPTER 10

God's 7 Feasts
The Appointed Times

Well, you made it! This is the final chapter entitled God's 7 Feasts - The Appointed Times. And this is where we're going to learn (finally!) what the phrase "no man knows the DAY or HOUR" is <u>REALLY</u> about! This is one of the most misunderstood Bible verses in today's church world. But I promise you, if you'll read this chapter, you'll know the full truth, the wonderful truth, behind these precious words!

Remember friend, it's all about a game! God created the Game of Life! And make no mistake about it ... God has laid out the timing scenario for the game from the very beginning, including when Jesus will return! We've learned in this book the game was/is set to be played for 6,000 solar years, followed by a bonus period of 1,000 solar years. Then God divided that 7,000 year total timeframe into seven equal periods of 1,000 years each [See Figure 11]. We learned God hid this time clock for the game in the 7 Day Creation story, by utilizing 6 days to create the world followed

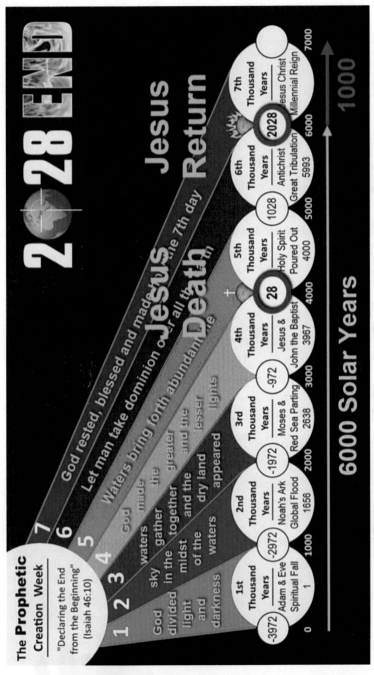

Figure 11 - God's Game of Life (7,000 Year) Plan

by a 7th day of rest. Each Creation day <u>foretold</u> of a future 1,000 year period. And each Creation Day contained a prophecy foretelling the greatest event to occur in its future millennium.

In addition to that, we learned God prophesied Jesus Christ would DIE for us (on the cross) during Earth's 4,000 year, and he will RETURN for us during earth's 6,000 year. On our Gregorian calendar today these years are AD 28 for his death and AD 2028 for his return. Then after Christ's return the 1,000 year bonus period will begin on Earth in fulfillment of the 7th Day Sabbath in the Creation story. The resurrected saints will live and reign with Christ for 1,000 years. It will be a time of holiness and rest on earth, just as God spoke about the Sabbath Day in the Creation story. So that's it! That's the timing scenario for the YEAR COUNT in God's Game of Life: 7,000 total years (6,000 + 1,000) – Jesus dies year 4,000 and returns year 6,000.

So what about the phrase "no man knows the DAY or HOUR"? What's it about? Well, for that we need to turn to God's 7 Feasts. The word "feast" is from the Hebrew word *mo'ed* meaning *"appointed times"* (Leviticus 23:1-4). Did you catch that? God's 7 Feasts are His appointed times! What's that mean? It means they're prophecy! God's 7 Feasts contain more information about the game clock in God's Game of Life. But they have nothing to do with the year count! Instead, they foretell the VERY **DAY** (not the year!) but the VERY **DAY** during a calendar year when certain things will happen! Specifically, God's 7 feasts foretell the VERY DAY when the Messiah (Christ Jesus) will accomplish his most important duties, including his death on the cross and his return at the sound of a trumpet!

So let's look at this ... God set up the yearly observance of His 7 Feasts with the Israelites (back in the wilderness) right after they escaped from Egypt. So it was roughly 1300 BC – over a thousand years before Jesus would arrive! These Feasts are written in Leviticus chapter 23. God gave the name of the feast, what it was to be about, and the very day it was to be observed each year based upon a lunar calendar. A lunar calendar means the months were based upon the moon cycle – each month started and ended with the new moon.

God commanded the Israelites to keep these 7 Feasts every year (just like we keep holidays today). In fact, the word "holiday" literally came from these Feasts, for they were also known as the "holy days", which forms the word "holiday". But just keep in mind, the Israelites had no clue these Feasts days (appointed times) were actually foretelling the EXACT DAY(S) when Jesus would accomplish his most important tasks. In fact, the very essence of what each feast was about was the very essence of what Jesus had to fulfill on that day! This is wonderful knowledge to understand!

So here are the Feasts in the order they arrive each year ...

  1. Feast of Passover
  2. Feast of Unleavened Bread
  3. Feast of First Fruits
  4. Feast of Weeks
  5. Feast of Trumpets

6. Day of Atonement
7. Feast of Tabernacles

The first 3 Feasts occurred in the spring over an 8 day period during the lunar month of Nissan. Passover was on the 14th, Unleavened Bread ran the next 7 days from the 15th to the 21st, and First Fruits occurred during the week of Unleavened Bread on the day after the weekly Sabbath [See Figure 12]. God declared the month of Nissan as the first month of the year on a religious calendar for the Jews.

The 4th Feast of the year (Feast of Weeks) was to take place 50 days (7 weeks + 1 day) after the Feast of First Fruits. So it arrived late spring, during the 3rd lunar month of the year, the month of Sivan.

The last 3 Feasts occurred in the fall, during the 7th lunar month of the year, the month of Tishri. Trumpets occurred on the 1st day of the month, Atonement on the 10th, and Tabernacles ran for 7 days from the 15th to the 21st. These 3 Feasts are known collectively as the fall feasts of the Lord.

So there you go … that's God's 7 Feasts along with the VERY DAY they were to be observed each year based on lunar months. So here's what happened …

The Jews were keeping these feasts every year for over a thousand years, and here comes Jesus along Earth's 4,000 year, and he DIES on the CROSS (he's sacrificed!) on the VERY DAY of the Feast of Passover (the 1st feast of the year). This feast memorialized the day the Israelites had sacrificed their Passover lamb back in Egypt the night of their exodus – Nissan 14th. So here's Jesus, and he's sacrificed on the VERY DAY of

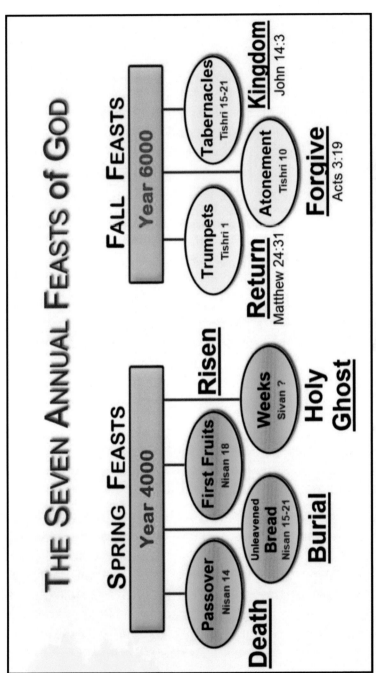

Figure 12 - The 7 Prophetic Feasts of Messiah

the Feast of Passover! He literally became the sacrificial Passover Lamb, fulfilling the Feast of Passover on its VERY DAY! This is the reason Paul wrote: "For Christ, our Passover Lamb, has been sacrificed" (I Corinthians 5:7). Wow!

By the way, the year Christ was crucified Nissan 14th fell on the 4th day of the week (sundown Tues to sundown Wed). So Christ hung on the cross on a Wednesday afternoon. I don't have time to go into detail on all these things in this book, but you can learn all these things (and much more) in the Moses chapter of my book "Undeniable Biblical Proof Jesus Christ Will Return to Planet Earth Exactly 2,000 Years After the Year of His Death".

Alright, so then Jesus' body was taken off the cross that same day (Nissan 14th) and it was buried in the ground at sundown, because the Jews wanted the bodies off the cross before the High Sabbath of the first day of Unleavened Bread arrived – Nissan 15th. Christ's body then remained in the ground for 3 days & 3 nights (Nissan 15 - 16 - 17) in fulfillment of the Jonah prophecy spoken by Christ in Matthew 12:40. So Jesus' body was in the ground (heart of the earth) all during the days of the Feast of Unleavened Bread! Christ's sinless body was the unleavened bread that fulfilled the feast!

Ok, so now we know Christ's death occurred the VERY DAY of the yearly celebrated Feast of Passover (the 1st feast of the year), and we know his burial took place during the VERY DAYS of the yearly celebrated Feast of Unleavened Bread (the 2nd feast of the year). Friend, these are the BIGGEST things Christ had to do for us to save us – his death and burial! So what about his resurrection?

Well, next came the Feast of First Fruits (the 3ʳᵈ feast of the year). Remember, it occurs right after the weekly Sabbath day ends during the 7 days of Unleavened Bread. So if you count 3 days and 3 nights from sundown Wednesday (when Christ's body was buried in the tomb) you come to sundown Saturday, which is the end of the weekly Sabbath! (The weekly Sabbath, the 7ᵗʰ day of the week, runs from sundown Friday to sundown Saturday.) So right on cue, Jesus resurrected from the grave on the VERY DAY of the Feast of First Fruits! Mary and Martha found the stone rolled away and the tomb empty early that Sunday morning while it was still dark. So here's the deal friend … Jesus literally became the First Fruits resurrection of the dead on the VERY DAY of the Feast of First Fruits. In other words, he fulfilled the purpose of the feast on its VERY DAY, just like the first 2 feasts! And this is why Paul wrote: "But now is Christ risen from the dead, and become the first fruits of them that slept" (I Corinthians 15:20). Wow!

So now you know Jesus fulfilled the spring feasts (the first 3 feasts of the year) – Passover, Unleavened Bread, and First Fruits – on their VERY yearly celebrated DAY(S) Earth's 4,000 year! The Messiah did his most important work for us (his death, burial, and resurrection) at God's appointed times, and no one knew it at the time. Mind boggling! But after Christ's resurrection he began to explain these things to his disciples. So they soon understood it!

Ok, so next came the Feast of Weeks (the 4ᵗʰ feast of the year). Remember this feast was to be kept 50 days after First Fruits. Well friend, this was the VERY DAY that Jesus sent the comforter, the Holy Ghost! Forty days after his resurrection Jesus ascended back into heaven, and 10 days later he poured out the Holy Ghost on his disciples! The church renamed this day "Pentecost", but the word "*Pentecost*" comes from the Greek word "*pentekostos*" meaning "fifty". That "50" is for the Feast of Weeks! Jesus sent the Holy Ghost in fulfillment of the Feast of Weeks! This feast memorialized the day God thunderously spoke the 10LC to the Israelites at Mt Sinai. I don't have time to get into it here, but friend the 10LC and the Holy Ghost are intimately linked. Read about it in the "Holy Spirit" chapter of my book "*Undeniable Biblical Proof Jesus Christ Will Return to Planet Earth Exactly 2,000 Years After the Year of His Death*"!

Alright, recapping where we're at … Jesus fulfilled his most important tasks (death, burial, resurrection, and sending Holy Ghost) on the VERY DAY(S) of God's first 4 feasts of the year – Passover, Unleavened Bread, First Fruits, and Weeks. So knowing this, let me ask you a question … there's 3 Feasts left, all occurring in the fall during the lunar month of Tishri (the 7ᵗʰ lunar month of the year) … do you think Jesus is going to do something important for us on the VERY DAY(S) of these 3 remaining fall feasts? OF COURSE HE IS!!! We would be foolish to not understand this once presented with it.

So the lasts 3 feasts are Trumpets, Atonement, and Tabernacles. Friend, this is exactly what Christ has left to do for us – return at the sound of a trumpet,

<u>officially</u> (priestly) atone for our sins, and then tabernacle with us (meaning live among us). Let me be clear … these 3 feasts are going to be fulfilled by Jesus Christ on their VERY DAY(S) all during Earth's 6,000 year, just like Jesus fulfilled the first 4 feasts on their very days all during Earth's 4,000 year! The Apostle Paul wrote: "Let no one judge you in regard to a feast (holy days), or a new moon, or Sabbaths, which are a SHADOW OF THINGS TO COME!" (Colossians 2:16-17). See, Paul knew the fall feasts still needed to be fulfilled! Pretty cool, huh?

So ok, if we know Jesus is returning on the VERY DAY of the Feast of Trumpets (the 5th feast of the year) then what about the phrase "no man knows the DAY or HOUR"? If he's returning on Trumpets, then how does this make sense? Friend, it's this simple … it's because the Feast of Trumpets is the only Feast day to occur at the start of a lunar month (the 1st day of the month), and this day was not known until 2 witnesses confirmed sighting of the new moon sliver to the Sanhedrin. This could happen at any HOUR of any DAY during the new moon phase which contains 3 days of darkness.

Eventually a Jewish idiom was coined, and the Feast of Trumpets became known as the Feast "no man knows the day or hour". They would have to "keep watch" for the Day of this Feast to arrive. And so you'll find Jesus using both these phrases when speaking of his return "no man knows the day or hour" and so "keep watch". It's tragic today the church thinks Jesus' phrase "no man knows the day or hour" is saying we will have no clue to the time of Christ's return, when in reality it's actually revealing the time of his return –

Feast of Trumpets!!! Isn't that shocking? It's sad how deceived an entire church generation can be!

For a decade now – ever since God gave me this 2028 END prophetic message back in 2008 – mostly what I hear is … "no man knows the day or hour" … "no man knows the day or hour" … "no man knows the day or hour." They're like parrots! Then they close their hearts and won't listen to a single word I say! Their "ears to hear" have been sealed shut by Satan, who has deceived them over this one phrase. It's heartbreaking!

But friend, listen to me … Jesus WANTS you to know the time of his return! He literally said, "KNOW that it is near, **EVEN RIGHT AT THE DOORS**" (Matthew 24:33). It was a direct command to us: **KNOW** when my return is right at the door! Well it will be "right at the door" Feast of Trumpets AD 2028, two thousand years after the year of his death (Passover AD 28) according to everything I've revealed in this book. It's just as the cover of my book has been proclaiming for a decade now … *"Jesus Christ Will Return to Planet Earth Exactly 2,000 Years After the Year of His Death"*.

Well alright, so let's wrap this up. God created the Game of Life. Planet Earth is the playing field, mankind is the players who will win or lose, and the 10LC are the rules. The game is being played by two teams – Jesus' team & Satan's team. If you play for Jesus' team, you will win the game. If you play for Satan's team, you will lose. The game was set to be played for 6,000 solar years, and then it will come to an end with Christ's return. After this, a 1,000 year bonus period will begin with Christ reigning on earth with all the resurrected saints. At the end of this 1,000 year period Satan will be released one last time to go out and deceive (if he can) all the new people who were born during this period. You can read how the game will wrap up in the final 3 chapters of the Game of Life's handbook (The Revelation 20, 21, & 22).

So here's the deal, my friend ... you only get a short time to play in the game! But every single play you run is being written down in books! Everything you think, speak, and do everyday of your life (every minute!) is being recorded. Jesus said: "But I say unto you, that every idle word that men shall speak, they shall give account thereof in the day of Judgment" (Matthew 12:36). Wow! The Game of Life's handbook says: "And I saw the dead, small and great, stand before God; and the books were opened: and another book was opened, which is the book of life: and the dead were judged out of those things which were written in the books, according to their deeds." (Revelation 20:12). Wow!

But friend, this is exactly what happens in the games we know and love here on Earth today! Take for example football, tennis, golf, hockey, etc ... every play every player makes is recorded in books. They know who did what, when, and where. In American football, they know a running back ran for 112 total yards – 23 yards in the first quarter on 4 carries. They know his first run was 7 yards on a 2nd down play to the left at the 2 min and 35 second mark of the game. In tennis, they know the winner served 22 aces, hit 144 backhands, ran for 1,786 meters, made 17 unforced errors, and on and on. Do you get it? Every play every player makes is recorded! Well likewise, <u>EVERYTHING</u> YOU DO in the Game of Life is being recorded! What you did! Where you did it! When you did it! Even why you did it, the motives of your heart!

So listen, on Judgment Day the evidence of your life will stand before you. It will be obvious what team you played on! Your works will prove it! If you ran plays of love, you'll enter into life in heaven; if you ran plays of pride, you'll perish in the lake of fire. So the choice is yours RIGHT NOW! You have the option RIGHT NOW to begin doing the things you need to do to win the Game! And make no mistake about it … if you're not playing for Jesus' team, you're playing for Satan's! There's no other option! You can't sit this game out! So I'm begging you, visit our all important website www.10LoveCommandments.com and watch "The Salvation Equation" video series and "The 10 Love Commandments" video series. These two seminars will clear up everything on how to win the Game of Life and receive the reward of eternal life.

I'm warning you … there are MANY false doctrines in today's churches (literally "doctrines from demons") meant to deceive you into living a lifestyle that ends in the lake of fire. So please, please, I cannot overstate how important it is for you to watch those two video seminars. Make sure you're playing for Jesus' team of love so you win the Game of Life!

Well that's it my friend. The first 6,000 years of God's Game of Life are almost over … it will END Feast of Trumpets 2028. God has purposed it! He has planned it! And He WILL bring it to pass! But don't wait till 2028 to get right with God, because He could pull you from the game tonight! So hit your knees and cry out to God, "Forgive me Lord, for every wicked thing

I've ever done!" And then get up, with a new heart, and a new spirit, and begin making the necessary changes in your life to play for Jesus' team. Well, I love you all! God help us! God bless.

The wicked will finally lose;
The righteous will finally win

(Proverbs 21:18, Living Bible)

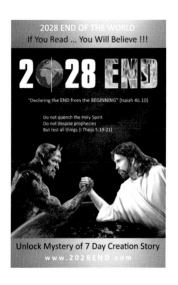

WITNESSING PACK # 1

12 - 2028 END Books (120 pgs each)
12 - Creation Brochures
12 - 10LC Bookmarks
 1 - 2028 END Blu-ray (280 min)
 1 - 2028 END DVD (280 min)

$50 (S&H included)

Send $50 check (or money order) to:

10 Love Commandments Ministries
PO Box 814
Nashville, TN 37076

Include shipping address and email address
(we will send shipping confirmation email)

We are making these items available to you at our cost
because we REALLY want you to be able to afford to purchase
these things to hand out to your family, friends, and church
congregation. May God bless you!

Or Order Online:
www.2028End.com/store/2028-end-book

UNDENIABLE
BIBLICAL
PROOF

JESUS CHRIST
WILL
RETURN
TO
PLANET
EARTH
EXACTLY
2,000
YEARS
AFTER
THE
YEAR
OF HIS
DEATH

WHAT YOU MUST DO TO BE READY!

GABRIEL ANSLEY

WITNESSING PACK #2

10 - UBP Books (408 pgs each)
30 - Creation Brochures
10 - 10LC Bookmarks
 1 - 2028 END Blu-ray (280 min)
 1 - 2028 END DVD (280 min)

$65 (S&H included)

USA Orders Only!

Send $65 check (or money order) to:

10 Love Commandments Ministries
PO Box 814
Nashville, TN 37076

Include shipping address and email address
(we will send shipping confirmation email)

We are making these items available to you at our cost
because we REALLY want you to be able to afford to purchase
these things to hand out to your family, friends, and church
congregation. May God bless you!

Or Order Online:
www.UndeniableBiblicalProof.com/order-book